CONTENTS

QUESTIONS ON GOD'S PROMISES

QUESTIONS ABOUT OUR FUTURE

QUESTIONS ANSWERS AND GOOD NEWS

HOPE FOR TODAY'S INQUIRING MINDS

Sharleen McTaggart

Questions Answers and Good News

Tellwell Talent
www.tellwell.ca

ISBN
978-0-2288-6681-7 (Paperback)
978-0-2288-6682-4 (eBook)

INTRODUCTION

You may be asking **w**hat in the world would a book with this name be all about?

My name is "Sharleen", and before we venture into this journey of questions, I just want to give you a heads up on why I began this adventure into writing and producing messages centered around questions and answers.

We are caught up in a wild and uncertain world these days. Would you have believed that we would be living in fear of catching a deadly virus, or that our world would be caught up in what many would describe as an economic catastrophe?

Would you have believed that many of your neighbours, or even you, would be out of work with no idea of just how long the shut down would last? Would you have believed that out of the many businesses forced to close down, many would never reopen, that sporting events you love to watch would be cancelled, or that movie houses, concert halls, entertainment venues would be off limits? Would you have ever believed you might lose your home or your car because of lost income or that your children would be home 24/7 for who knows how long? Would you have believed that protests, riots, and anger between ethnic groups would be so high and that the police would lose their title as our protectors

First let me assure you that I am not here to criticize or condemn, but merely to confirm the sorry state of our world and to point out the chaos all around us.

This situation has not only created fear, but it has caused many people to ask a great many questions. Questions that are asked by people like you and me and that you don't often hear addressed by the mainstream media. Questions I hope to deal with in a way that not only provides answers but that brings hope and good news amid the chaos.

I'm looking for people who will open their minds and hearts to hear and believe that there is hope, and we are not alone. Like Michael Heiser, a Hebrew Scholar I follow said in his opening podcast "I want to mold your worldview and lead you to learn something you may not have heard before but that will encourage and build you up no matter your present-day situation."[1]

Rather than spend a lot of time talking about myself in this introduction, I prefer to ask you to wait until chapter three in answer to the question, "Is there an answer to personal chaos?" to hear my story.

I will be providing most Scripture references in their entirety as it's not always convenient for you, the reader, to go to a Bible and check out the text. Yet, I think it's vital you know what it says, not just what I say it says!

BASIC QUESTIONS

I've been a faithful member of YouTube and its audience for almost 10 years, but as of late, I've noticed a preponderance of "bad news" on the platform and felt led to share my thoughts on what we might consider a *Good News* way to deal with all the chaos in our world.

There are a variety of places you can go to see just how many serious issues we are facing but here is a few:

- Armies of locusts spreading from Africa to India, and now even being seen in South America and Russia
- Extreme bizarre weather patterns
- Unprecedented flooding and fires
- Major earthquakes
- Unusual volcanic eruptions all over the globe
- A number of what might be called plagues that include African Swine Fever and a new rabbit virus
- Covid-19 and its variants
- Unprecedented economic problems
- Crime and what could soon be called revolutions everywhere including Hong Kong and the U.S.
- And recent rumors of possible armed conflicts involving China and the U.S., Iran and Israel; China and India; North and South Korea; and Russia and the Ukraine

And if that isn't enough to cause concern there is also an exponential rise in:

- opioid use causing death
- suicides
- murder rates all over Canada and the United States
- rampant homelessness

- a spike in the number of single-mother households
- the possibility of upcoming food shortages
- and the list goes on and on.

Although that's not where I want to put our focus, I feel it's important to be reminded, our world is in trouble.

Let's look at some questions I believe must be on the hearts and minds of many.

How can we not have questions in the face of such tragedies, sadness and fear all over our planet?

In each chapter of this book, I will deal with at least one question that I've heard asked and hope it will help you see that there is *Good News* amid the chaos.

Thirty-Two years ago, I was drowning in personal bad news so I can relate to how you might be feeling. Since that time, I have had questions, and most likely will continue to have questions, but I hope the answers I've found so far will bring you comfort and encouragement. Let's Begin…

Question #1

IS ANYONE IN CONTROL?

I actually typed that question into Google and came out with a variety of answers none of which made me feel safer or gave me an answer that could be considered "good news."

For example: are governments, politicians, bureaucrats, internet providers, science, bankers, despots, cartels, the media, Hollywood, radical extremists, secret societies, or cabals such as the Bilderberg Group, the Illuminati or Free Masons in control? Maybe it's powerful and wealthy families or corporations, educators or countries with the most ruthless leaders and grandest armies or, new to the list AI or high-tech companies

Do any of these options help you feel better about the state of our world today or where we might be headed? I would suggest not!

So here is the *good news* answer to this very important first question. *Yes, there is Someone in control!*

There is a Creator who has existed from the beginning of time and space and created everything we see here on earth and in the universe. In the late 90's, my husband and I were introduced to the teachings of an amazing scholar and scientist, Dr. Hugh Ross, as he was being interviewed on a local television network. Much of what I learned from his teaching has influenced my belief that yes, there is a Creator. Let's take a few minutes to consider some facts concerning our world.

With the help of the Hubble Telescope, science has shown us the universe is 13.79 billion years old and the earth is 4.5 billion years old. It has also discovered there are around 50 billion trillion stars that make their home in the observable universe. My friends, there is so much that science has discovered for us. As you read, this quote from Dr. Ross's book *Why the Universe Is the Way It Is* please note the term "just-right."

"The mass of the universe is fine-tuned to provide two life-essential features simultaneously: (1) the just-right amounts and diversity of elements and (2) the just-right expansion rates throughout cosmic history so that certain types of stars and planets form at the just-right times and in the just-right locations. Fine tuning to provide two life-essential characteristics at once hints louder than a whisper at purposeful design."[1]

That this fine-tuning, far exceeds our best human achievements implies that the causal Agent Who designed these features for the existence and benefit of human beings is, at minimum, many orders of magnitude more intelligent, knowledgeable, inventive, creative and powerful than humans. Since intellect, knowledge, inventiveness, creativity and power are attributes that only a personal being can possess, the causal Agent Who created the universe must be a personal being.

This is the being we hear about in the very first verse of the Bible.:

> *In the beginning, God created the heavens and the earth."–*
> *Genesis 1:1*

So based on science, let's take a leap of faith and consider that there is a God, and He is in control.

I don't know about you, but for me that is *good news!* With all the questions we might have as we consider the state of our world, I am

---

[1] Hugh Ross, *Why the Universe Is the Way It Is*, printed in the United States of America, October 2008, Published by Baker Books, Page 35

reassured that there is Someone far bigger and way smarter than anyone we might have been inclined or persuaded to put our faith in, Who is in control.

Please do your homework and check out this amazing website "www.reasons.org" and then come back for another question we can look at again always looking for good news answers to challenging questions.

Question #2

WHERE CAN I GO TO GET ANSWERS?

In Chapter One, we looked at the question, *Is anyone in control?* I hope you were encouraged to hear that yes, there is, the Creator God of the Universe, and we looked at how this wonderful truth is supported and confirmed by science.

So, it seems the next relevant question might be, "*Where can I go to get answers about this Creator God that are reliable and trustworthy?*"

Let's begin by reflecting on some amazing statistics about the book I suggest is the only true source of those answers—the Bible.

Did you know that according to Guiness World Records,[2] there were five billion copies (as of 1995) in print with over 100 million copies printed each year? It is easily the most read book in the world.

It is not a book that arrived in a complete form at one single point in history. Although it is viewed as one book, it is actually a compilation of 66 books written by 40 Authors on 3 continents from 1500 B.C. to 100 A.D. in 3 original languages of Hebrew, Aramaic and Greek.

It is called *God's Word* even though God did not physically write it. Instead, He worked through everyday people, inspired by Him, to record what we accept as the Bible. The Old Testament is primarily a record of God creating the world and His dealings with the Hebrews or Jews. The New Testament continues the record with first century accounts of the life and ministry of Jesus and the struggles faced by

---

2 En.wikipedia.org/wiki/List_of_best_selling_books

new Christians in a hostile culture. There are also a variety of subjects and literary elements included, history, the writings of the Major and Minor Prophets, poetry, prophecy, letters and of course the Gospels that include Jesus' own words.

The Bible I've used since February 1990 is the New International Translation that was compiled by over 100 scholars working directly from the best Hebrew, Aramaic and Greek texts. It is noted that the first concern of the translators was the accuracy of the translation and its fidelity to the thought of the biblical writers. In the preface of this Bible there are 3 pages of information relating to this process that is reassuring as to its accuracy. The preface—the very first place a new reader should begin—shows how what you're about to study was compiled.

There are 2 Bible verses I'd like to share with you that affirm the Bible as trustworthy and true. One from the Old Testament found in

> *2 Samuel 22: 31, "As for God, his way is perfect; the word of the Lord is flawless"*

and one from the New Testament spoken by Jesus himself from

> *John 17:17, "Sanctify them by the truth; your word is truth."*

And when the Apostle John was writing the last book of the Bible, he was told by God in

> *Revelation 21:5, "Write this down, for these words are trustworthy and true."*

You may be thinking that is all well and good but is there any proof, outside of the Bible itself? That is why, in this chapter, I'd like to provide information that will help you believe what is contained in this book is true and there is an abundance of evidence for that statement that takes many forms.

Proof #1: we have copies of the original manuscripts and throughout history, these copies show that the Bible has been transmitted accurately. Despite common skeptical claims that the Bible has often been changed through the centuries, the physical evidence tells another story. You could go to *The Archeological Study Bible*[3] and see many notes and articles documenting how archeology has again and again proven that the Bible does correspond to historical reality. For example, clay tablets dating to 2300 B.C. have been found in Syria strongly supporting Old Testament stories, vocabulary and geography. Consider this—skeptics doubted the existence of the Hittites from Genesis chapters 15, 20, and 49 until a Hittite city, complete with records, was found in Turkey. There are dozens of other Old Testament facts supported by similar discoveries.

More importantly, no facts presented in the Old or New Testaments have been shown to be false. This historical reliability is crucial to our trust in those statements I shared earlier, statements taken from Scripture.

Proof #2: Accurate copying is also an important factor in the Bible's reliability. New Testament writings were composed within a few decades of the actual events they describe, far too early for legend or myth to overtake actual history. Historians have access to a tremendous number of manuscripts, proving the New Testament was reliably and quickly copied and distributed. This gives ample confidence that what we read today correctly represents the original writing.

Old Testament writings also show an abundance of evidence of being reliably transmitted, from when the Dead Sea Scrolls were discovered in the 1940's in the caves of Qumran. They were 800 years older than any other available manuscripts. Comparing earlier and later manuscripts showed a meticulous approach to transmission, once again adding to our confidence that what we have today represents the original texts.

---

3 *An illustrated Walk Through Biblical History* published in 2005 by Zondervan

The Bible has more empirical support which is a shorter time between original writing and surviving copies, and a greater number of source manuscripts than any other ancient work by far.

For example, there are only 250 copies of the works of Julius Caesar, the earliest from 950 years *after* they were written, with no way to know how well those copies represent the originals.

In comparison, for the New Testament, there are currently 5,000 manuscripts, with the earliest copies anywhere from 200 to 300 years later and some less than 100 years later. This gives a better than 99 percent confidence in the contents of the original text.

In short, we not only have objective reasons to claim the Bible is reliable, but we cannot call it unreliable without throwing out almost everything else we know of ancient history. If the Scriptures don't pass a test for trustworthiness, no records from that era can. The Bible's reliability is proven in both its historical accuracy and its accurate transmission.

In closing this chapter, I want to share with you a well-known example of where the Bible has made a claim that science is only now beginning to recognize and how amazing it is that with the new "Hubble Telescope" technology and the present location of the planets, stars, galaxies at just the right place, scientists can actually see back to the beginning of time.

Although the Bible claims the universe had a beginning, philosophers and scientists rejected that claim for over 2000 years, but now astronomers have proven the universe indeed had a beginning, the so-called big bang described as the greatest scientific proof of the inerrancy of the Bible.

For those of you who are inclined to want answers to other specific situations in Scripture that perhaps only scientific discoveries can address, I again suggest you go to www.reasons.org and dig in!

Dr. Hugh Ross, the founder of this site, holds a degree of physics, a PhD in Astronomy and in 2012 together with Dr. Gerald Schroeder received the Trotter Prize presented by Texas A&M University in recognition of his work in demonstrating connections between Science and Religion.

I remember hearing Dr. Ross share how he came to believe not only in God, but in the Christian God of the Bible. He was a young man who was very much into science, especially Astronomy, and not a believer in God. At one point, he decided to investigate if there was anywhere he could go to find out if there was a God. So, he chose to read all the "holy books" of the world religions such as Islam, Buddhism, Hinduism, Sikhism and of course the Bible. From these investigations, he was greatly convinced that most of their writings were in no way provable scientifically until he picked up a Bible. He said from the very first chapters of Genesis, which describe the creation of the world, he knew this Book was true. Why? Because the Biblical days of creation fit the scientific model exactly. From that point forward, he read the rest of God's Word with a belief in its reliability which led him to trust in the God of Christianity and dedicate his life to comparing scientific findings with Biblical teaching and has over these many years found there to be no false teachings in the Bible.

So, we *do* have another Good News Answer to help us cope with the disturbing issues of our day.

> First—there is a Creator God who is in control
>
> Second—we have a reliable and trustworthy place to find out about Him and to see what answers there are for us that can be considered Good News.

In the next chapter I'd like to share with you another Good News Answer to the Question – *Is there an answer to Personal Chaos?*

Question #3

IS THERE AN ANSWER TO PERSONAL CHAOS?

MY STORY

Let me begin by asking the questions, *Is the news getting any better? Are things calming down?* I would say the answer to both questions is *no.* As a matter of fact, the chaos is escalating, and questions that need answers are increasing.

In the first two chapters, we looked at good news answers to two very important questions, *is anyone in control?* We found there is, the Creator God of the Universe. And *where can I go to get reliable and trustworthy information about Him?* I hope you were comforted to hear that there is, the Bible.

Today, I'm switching my focus to good news in times of personal chaos. To do that, I will share my story. My goal in sharing with you is to help you see where I came from and where I've been, and through my journey, you might see yourself somewhere in my life. Most importantly I pray you will see how God and the Bible helped me deal with my personal times of chaos. In other words, I'm going to share my Good News experience.

I know that book learning is good, and I have some of that too, but the saying "Been there, done that, got the T-Shirt" means so much more when you're looking for sage advice. When you hear that the person sharing with you had a fair amount of chaos in her life but fortunately received answers to many of her questions, may you be encouraged and enlightened. Life is filled with challenges, struggles, problems, and questions. Maybe I can help. I will now begin with my history.

I am a woman, daughter, wife, stepmother, grandmother, sister-in-law, daughter-in-law, neighbor, and friend.

I have lived in a variety of settings including at a farm, in a small village, in a small town, and on an island in the Atlantic, in a number of large cities, in a rural senior's lifestyle community and now, I am back in my hometown.

My homes have included a farmhouse, every type of apartment you can imagine, a townhouse, a luxury condo, a duplex, a triplex, single family dwellings both large and small, and a lovely mobile home.

My work took me from Ontario to Manitoba to Bermuda to Ontario and to British Columbia. Retirement brought me back to Ontario.

I have been employed as a waitress, an assembly line worker, a bank teller, a legal secretary, a finance company manager, a business owner, a counsellor in the correctional justice system and a Salvation Army Officer. Now I am blissfully and busily retired.

I have been single, married, divorced, common-law, married, separated and happily reunited once again with the love of my life the last 45 years.

I've dealt with issues such as being picked on as a child—now referred to as bullying, been involved in the abuse of alcohol and drugs over a period of 20 years, been a grateful cancer survivor, and been in a variety of other situations that could have led to a life destroyed.

That leads me to my new career as an author and YouTuber/podcaster with a heart that wants to help people who may see themselves in my life. You see, I am pretty ordinary, really, but finding Good News Answers to life's problems has led me to understand that those answers are worth sharing with others, even though the issues we are facing may seem much, much bigger.

Now, I would like to share with you a message I prepared to share with people who come across my path whom I feel can be helped. I believe therefore, in this upside-down world, it fits in with the overall theme of this book *Questions, Answers, and Good News.*

Now, to my actual story.

My life up to age 41 is summed up by wild living and self-destructive behavior. On the outside, I was looking okay, as a matter of fact, many would have said I had it all together, but on the inside, I was empty and searching for answers. It had become apparent that my lifestyle and determination to succeed were not going to help me reach the places I longed and hoped for.

Growing up with religion, I considered myself a Christian because in my early years, I attended church regularly with my mother and would have said that I believed in God, even though for 30 years I didn't give Him much thought. For as long as I could remember, I felt there had to be something more. As my life began to unravel, I started searching for answers in horoscopes, transcendental meditation, self-help books, positive thinking tapes and so on. However, these attempts came up short.

Things only changed when I cried out to God, "If you're real, I need help." Within minutes, I felt led to look for a church and I began my journey toward healing and becoming a new creation. I started to listen to teachings from the Bible that spoke to me personally, read a lot of books about God, and finally started reading the Bible on my own. I was right; there was something more.

What I did not know was that my rebellion was first toward God. The Bible calls it sin. I discovered that the love and acceptance I was longing for was only available in being reconciled to Him. What I really needed only Jesus could give me. My journey toward a personal relationship with God reached a turning point. I remember the moment I could not go on any longer. I stopped searching in all the wrong places and spread my arms in complete surrender to Jesus, giving Him my life, no matter what He wanted to do with it—I was never the same again!

My journey to healing culminated in a similar experience for my husband in less than a year with freedom for him from serious alcohol and drug abuse. Did our lives change? Absolutely. Our marriage and family relationships were repaired, and our lives absolutely turned around.

I share my story with you, trusting that if you have questions, problems, trials, or tribulations, you will reach out to my God, the Creator of the Universe, Who is just waiting for you to come to Him. Because of what the Lord Jesus Christ has done for me, I am compelled to encourage others to seek Him, receive His grace and mercy, and to know Him personally. How about you?

If you want to know about Jesus and how you can have a personal relationship with Him, I say to you just what I believe God said to me at my time of need, *"My child, I love you. Come to Me, read My Word"* and claim this promise found in 2 Corinthians like I did *"If anyone is in Christ, he is a new creation; the old has gone, the new has come!" 2 Corinthians 5:17*

I hope you can see how my choices in a time of chaos brought me peace and contentment. As we continue to hear all the bad news—the escalation of turmoil around our world—I hope that you will hear God's call to come to Him.

In the next section of this book, we will look at a question I often hear asked: *If God is in control, how come there is so much evil in our world?*

QUESTIONS ON THE ORIGIN OF OUR PROBLEMS

Question # 4 - Rebellion Part 1

WHY IS THERE SO MUCH EVIL IN OUR WORLD?

This question seems to arise even more often today as we see our world of chaos growing ever more frightening.

After being encouraged by the good news that there is Someone in control, the Creator God of the Universe, and then being provided with substantial proof that we can find out about Him in the Bible, a place that is reliable and trustworthy. Now we move along to this very important answer that I believe will be a real eye-opener to most readers.

> *"If God is in control, how come there is so much evil and turmoil in our world today?"*

The answer to this question will take four chapters to unpack properly, so I hope you are with me for the long haul.

We will start at the beginning, jump to the end, and then journey through three very important events in the history of mankind to see God's plan in action. By the way, that is the Good News in all of this—*God has a plan*—that begins in the Garden of Eden in the book of Genesis and ends in the new Garden of Eden in the book of Revelation.

This study will cover some things you may not have heard before and for some, it will help you relearn some things in a fresh way.

First, we see that in a certain way, this is God's story and how He cares for His creation. Think of it this way. Is it a normal part of our nature to care about the things we make and hold as important to us? The God of the Bible shares this profile. You see, God did not create humanity because He lacked something. He was not lonely, as though He was incomplete or needed company. God needs nothing because, well, *He's God.* He created things to enjoy the work of His own hands, so to speak. And the things He cares about most are those He made to be like Himself, in his own image (Genesis 1:26). That would be you and me.

We are here because God wanted us here and created us, the Bible refers to Him as our "Father." People from Adam onward are referred to as His children, but to really understand the context for the family-centered language in the Bible, we need to go back to the time before God made the earth and the human race.

It may surprise you, but God was not alone then either. That is another reason why we can be sure He didn't create us to heal His own loneliness. The Bible tells us that before God created us, He had already created other intelligent beings and called them "sons of God." Now we call them angels. The Old Testament book of Job tells us that God made it clear to Job that the sons of God "shouted for joy" when He laid the foundations of the earth.

> *"Where were you when I laid the earth's foundation? Tell me, if you understand. Who marked off its dimensions? Surely you know! Who stretched a measuring line across it? On what were its footings set, or who laid its cornerstone – while the morning stars sang together and all the* ***sons of God*** *shouted for joy." –Job 38:4-7*

You see, they were already present and watching their Father God at work.

They were actually God's heavenly or supernatural family—He the Father, and they the sons. God is Father to the intelligent beings He created in an unseen realm as well as to us.

The fact that God already had a supernatural family helps us understand His motivation for the creation of Adam and Eve, the first humans in the Genesis story. You see, God wanted a human family, in addition to His supernatural family. Incredibly, the story of Eden tells us God wanted His two families to live together in His presence. This means that just like the angels, humans were originally created fit for the presence of God Himself. Let's dig a little deeper to see how we know that.

The first book of the Bible, Genesis, begins with creation. God had done a lot of creating by the time the story gets to Adam and Eve. We are shown God creating the universe, planets, stars, plants, insects, flying creatures and land animals, but none of those creatures, could have a relationship or converse with God. They could not share their thoughts or express their appreciation to Him. As spectacular as plants and animals are, they couldn't play the role of children. They were not family. That is what God really wanted. He then chose to create something like Himself, as I shared earlier, new creatures in His image and likeness. They would be His earthly family.

So, what does "image" mean and why is it important? Think of the "image of God" as a verb, and you are on the right track to understanding the idea. We were created to image God, to be His imagers, to represent Him. We can actually see what that looks like in

> *Genesis 1: 27-28 (ESV), "So God created man in His own image, in the image of God he created him; male and female he created them. And God blessed them. And God said to them, "Be fruitful and multiply and fill the earth and subdue it and have dominion over the fish of the sea and over the birds of the heavens and over every living thing that moves on the earth."*

You see, He created an earthly family to assume His role in managing and maintaining His new creation. They would be understudies and partners. Imaging God means being God's representation on earth. God tasked humans with doing a job He could just as well have done Himself. But He wanted His children to participate. You see, Eden was not merely God's home; it was God's home office. We were created to be God's co-workers.

To make sure the people He made could do the job of imaging Him on earth, He shared his attributes, qualities and abilities with them, things like intelligence and creativity. He made us like Him so we could participate with Him, as co-rulers and co-caretakers in His new world. Have you ever wondered if you have a purpose or a mission in life? Wonder no more! Every person, no matter how small or weak or short-lived has some role to play in someone else's life. What we do matters and most of the time in small, unspectacular ways.

Now to the bad news of how something happened to ruin God's plan, right in the very beginning. As a matter of fact, the heartache would be so great that God almost decided to give up on humanity—a few times!

Remember I told you how God shared His attributes with His first human creation and as wonderful as that was and is, this is where things get interesting and scary. One of God's attributes is freedom, what we often call free will. So, here's part one of the Bible's answer to that question, *why is there evil in the world*? That answer is the attribute of free will.

God made the same decision earlier with the heavenly family He had created. They had abilities like intelligence and freedom as well, gifts from their Creator, and this is what transpired:

One of God's supernatural children decided to dishonour God's decision to have a human family by tempting Eve, hoping God would destroy her and Adam. He came to Eve in the form of a serpent Genesis 3:1 (NIV),

> *"Now the serpent was more crafty than any of the wild animals, the LORD God had made. He said to the woman."*

How do we know the serpent was part of God's heavenly family? The Bible refers to the serpent as Satan and the Devil in Revelation 12:9 (NIV),

> *"The great dragon was hurled down—that ancient serpent called the devil, or Satan, who leads the whole world astray."*

He did succeed, in getting Eve to disobey God—to sin. However, when it came to getting rid of humanity permanently, the devil failed.

It is also important for us to recognize, that God rejected the idea of creating humans as robots or preprogrammed computers made of flesh. Without the genuine freedom to make real decisions, we simply would not be like God. Without genuine free will, we cannot authentically love or obey God. For decisions like love and obedience to be authentic, they must be made against a truly possible alternative.

The result of all this is that evil exists because people abuse God's wonderful gift of freedom and use it for self-gratification, revenge, and selfish desires. This rebellion began in Eden.

But what happened in Eden was only the beginning of the story. As a result, God kicked Adam and Eve out of His house and in Genesis 3:22-23 (NIV) we hear why,

> *"The man has now become like one of us (sons of god) knowing good and evil. He must not be allowed to reach out his hand and take also from the tree of life and eat and live forever. So the LORD God banished him from the Garden of Eden to work the ground from which he has been taken."*

Then He cursed the serpent Genesis 3: 14-15

> *"So the LORD God said to the serpent, 'Because you have done this, 'Cursed are you above all the livestock and all the wild animals.'"*

And then He cast him away from His presence—to the earth. (Isaiah 14:12)

> *"How you have fallen from heaven, O morning star, son of the dawn! You have been cast down the earth."*

The message was forceful and simple: Rebellion #1 would be punished.

You would think everyone would get the message. Not so, things got even worse as we will see next in Part two of this answer. Rebellion #2 is another cause of the evil permeating our world.

Please do not be discouraged, that it does not seem like there is much good news so far in this series. The answer to the question *"Why is there so much evil in our world"* has to be dealt with as "bad news" and Part two of this answer will also seem like *more* bad news but hang in there, good news is on the horizon!

Question # 4 - Rebellion Part 2

WHY IS THERE SO MUCH EVIL IN OUR WORLD?

Welcome to Part 2 as we look at the answer to the question *"If God is in control, why is there so much evil in our world."*

As I shared before, this question will take me 4 chapters to answer. Reason #1 began in Genesis chapter 3 back in the Garden of Eden, the place where being estranged from God and ultimately experiencing death all began as we are reminded in *Romans 6:23, "The wages of sin is death."* Originally, we were *not* meant to die. If only Adam and Eve had trusted God and resisted the devil's schemes.

The result of all this is that evil exists because people abused God's wonderful gift of freedom, and as we will see, this doesn't end in the Garden. I'd like to interject here that God saw what was coming and we will see His amazing, good news answer in Chapter 5.

But first, we must examine two more events that plunged humanity further into the depths of depravity and chaos. The second of these which we will look at today is described in *Genesis 6:1-4* an incident many overlook or misunderstand:

> *"When man began to increase in number on the earth and daughters were born to them, the sons of God saw that the daughters of men were beautiful, and they married any of them they chose" NIV.*

The story in Genesis chapter 6 is about how some of God's supernatural children the "sons of God" wanted to imitate God by producing their own human children to image themselves. They decided to use women, the "daughters of man," for that purpose. This actually made them rivals to God, their own heavenly Father. Rather than be happy with God's desire to have humans become members of their family, they decided they wanted to be overlords of these humans.

We also see references in the New Testament to these rebellious "angels" in

> *2 Peter 2:4 (NIV), "For if God did not spare angels when they sinned, but sent them to hell, putting them into gloomy dungeons to be held with judgment."* and in *Jude 1:6 (NIV), "And the angels who did not keep their positions of authority but abandoned their own home—these he has kept in darkness, bound with everlasting chains for judgment on the great day."*

We see the result of their disobedience when God sent them to hell, but the deed was done, and it had disastrous consequences as we see in

> *Genesis 6:5-6 (NIV), "The LORD saw how great man's wickedness on the earth had become, and that every inclination of the thoughts of his heart was only evil all the time. The LORD was grieved that he had made man on the earth, and his heart was filled with pain."*

This rebellion took the effects of sin to another level, accelerating human self-destruction. Humanity had been permanently damaged. I'd like to share some important information relating to just how much damage Rebellion #2 created for mankind – how much evil they brought into our world.

In Genesis 6: 5, we see one of the Bible's most vivid descriptions of total depravity:

> *"The LORD saw how great the man's wickedness on the earth had become, and that every inclination of the thoughts of his heart was only evil all the time."*

And then 5 verses later, in (verses 11 and 12), that description was expanded upon

> *"Now the earth was corrupt in God's sight and full of violence. God saw how corrupt the earth had become, for all the people on earth had corrupted their ways."*

That seems pretty clear, doesn't it? The second rebellion was devastating. Although these statements in the Bible are essentially, a summary of the effect of the transgression, if we look into the later Second Temple Jewish literature, we find much more detail.

First Enoch 8 (qbible.com/enoch/8)[4] goes on to elaborate, how certain "watchers," another term for "sons of God," corrupted humankind, by means of the sharing of forbidden, divine knowledge. In other words, teaching humanity to destroy themselves by leading them into idolatry and by teaching them skills and technologies of warfare. They were also taught all about growing herbs to intoxicate themselves as well as lessons on astrology and arts of seduction to proliferate immorality. In essence, these rebels kick started human destruction. I would say, that provides a pretty good overview of evil that is ultimately with us, even today, as is the influence of "false gods."

In Genesis 7 verse 17, we see that God saw no other solution but to send the flood to wipe out humanity.

> *"I am going to bring floodwaters on the earth to destroy all life under the heavens, every creature that has the breath of life in it. Everything on earth will perish."*

He decided the only choice was to start over and put an end to what the rebellious "sons of God" had caused and that only one man was said to be righteous in God's eyes—Noah. Verse 22 says,

> *"Noah did everything just as God commanded him."*

---

4 http://qbible.com.enoch/8.html

In Genesis 9:1 after the flood, God repeated the original commands He had given to Adam and Eve back in Genesis 1:22,

> *"Be fruitful and multiply and fill the earth"*.

God was starting over with them and added to that He made a covenant (a promise) to never destroy humanity with a flood ever again. Amazingly, God still wanted a human family. Not as amazing, but still pretty incredible, the abuse of God's goodness would continue.

Part three on rebellion in the next chapter shows how God's decision in part two frames the rest of the biblical story, and how once again we see God's unconquerable patience. Even as we continue to focus on what might appear as bad news, the good news of God's love shines through.

Question #4 - Rebellion Part 3

WHY IS THERE SO MUCH EVIL IN THE WORLD?

So far we have discussed Rebellion #1 – that involved a serpent who was originally Lucifer, one of God's spiritual children, also known as Satan, who rebelled against Him in leading Adam and Eve into sin. The result was the closing of the Garden of Eden and the Tree of Life to God's human family and that mankind would from that point forward experience death.

We then looked at Rebellion #2 – that involved a number of God's spiritual children (referred to as the sons of God) who in Genesis 6:1-4 left the spiritual realm and united themselves with women here on earth, which would ultimately lead to God bringing judgment in the form of a The Flood upon the earth.

So now, what appears to be approximately 400 years forward we come to Rebellion #3, the Tower of Babel.

Like the stories of Adam and Eve and Noah's flood, you may have heard of the Tower of Babel. If not, that's okay, because even most churchgoers don't realize what really happened.

The story of the Tower of Babel is found in Genesis 11:1-9,

> *"Now the whole world had one language and a common speech. As men moved eastward, they found a plain in Shinar and settled there. They said to each other, 'Come, let's make bricks and bake them thoroughly.' They used brick instead of stone, and tar for mortar. Then they said,*

'Come, let us build ourselves a city, with a tower that reaches to the heavens, so that we may make a name for ourselves and not be scattered over the face of the whole earth. But the LORD came down to see the city and the tower the people were building. The LORD said 'If as one people speaking the same language they have begun to do this, then nothing they plan to do will be impossible for them. Come, let us go down and confuse their language so they will not understand each other.' So the LORD scattered them from there over all the earth, and they stopped building the city. That is why it was called, Babel—because there the LORD confused the language of the whole world. From there the LORD scattered them over the face of the whole earth.'"

Now, you may remember that after the flood God wanted Noah's descendants to multiply and spread out over the earth with the instruction to be fruitful and increase in number and fill the earth. Here we see that they were certainly not filling the earth. Matter of fact, they were congregating in one place with a totally different agenda.

Like Adam and Eve, they were supposed to be God's co-workers (imagers) to maintain creation. Instead of doing that, they gathered at a place called Babel and built a tower for their own glory.

Now that's the familiar version of the story, but further significance is found in two unfamiliar verses in another biblical book.

Deuteronomy 32:8-9 (ESV) says,

"When the Most High gave to the nations their inheritance, when He divided mankind, he fixed the borders of the peoples according to the number of the sons of God. But the LORD's portion is His people. Jacob His allotted heritage."

These two verses tell us that one of the judgments at the Tower of Babel was the division of humankind. Up until this point in the story, God was dealing with humanity as a collective whole. That changed at Babel. Human beings would be segregated by language and geography.

Even worse, God in a sense divorced himself from humanity. Fed up with human defiance of His will, (another way of saying REBELLION), God assigned the nations of the earth to the oversight of other members of His supernatural family—the sons of God. This was a different group than those who transgressed before the flood.

You see, God couldn't kick humanity out of His house. He had done that already, back in Eden.

He had promised not to destroy humanity after the flood, and there would be no repeat of that disaster. So, what else could He do? He essentially said, "Enough! If you don't want me to be your God, I'll assign you to some of my heavenly assistants."

The fallout of this judgment took many forms. We aren't told how long it took, but the Bible tells us that the supernatural sons of God assigned over the nations did a lousy job.

Listen to how they became corrupt in (*Psalm 82: 1-5)* so corrupt that God had to judge them, too.

> "*God presides in the great assembly; he renders judgment among the 'gods': 'How long will you defend the unjust and show partiality to the wicked? Defend the weak and fatherless; uphold the cause of the poor and oppressed. Rescue the weak and needy; deliver them from the hand of the wicked. The 'gods' know nothing, they understand nothing. They walk about in darkness; all the foundations of the earth are shaken.*'"

Then we hear how He would one day take away their immortality and take back the nations in (*verses 6-8).*

> *"I said 'You are "gods", you are all sons of the Most High. But you will die like mere mortals, you will fall like every other ruler.'"*

For our purposes here, God's frustration left Him childless in terms of having a human family. He'd had it, but had he given up? Well, not quite. You see there was no Plan B.

Guess what happened right after the Tower of Babel catastrophe? God appeared to Abram, an old man married to Sarah who was beyond the age where she could have children. God made a covenant with Abram. He promised the old man and his wife that they would have a son. God would do a miracle. Their son would be the beginning of a new family for God on earth. I would suggest you read all about it in Gen 12:1-9; 15: 1-6; 18:1-15.

Having allotted humanity to the oversight of members of his heavenly host, God chose to begin anew with a family of his own, referred to as the Lord's Portion in Deuteronomy 32:9, with Abram. Abram believed God's promises. Note how this relationship between God and Abram started with God. All Abram had to do was believe, to have faith which we see he did in Genesis 15:6 *"Abram believed the LORD, and he credited it to him as righteousness."*

Promising Abram a son and through him, the start of a new family that would grow into a great nation was God's second covenant after the disaster of Eden. The first had been with Noah. Both were designed to preserve His dream of having a human family. You see God had not given up on humanity. He couldn't stop loving people. He still wanted a human family and Abram's family would become known as Israel, the name most frequently used in the Old Testament for God's human family.

But, what about the people from the other nations, the ones God had assigned to the sons of God after the Tower of Babel rebellion? They are called "Gentiles" in the Bible a short term that means "not from Israel". And despite what happened at Babel, God did not forget about these people. Actually, He told Abram that his descendants would someday be a blessing to the other nations God had forsaken. Genesis 12:3 says,

> *"I will bless those who bless you, and whoever curses you I will curse; and all peoples on earth will be blessed through you."*

Throughout the rest of the Old Testament, we do see that Gentiles could join God's family by choosing to reject all other gods, believing in Him alone.

It would be great to say that all went well from then on for Israel, but that would not be true. "The Lord's portion" wasn't a pretty one. They were God's people, but sadly, perhaps predictably, their loyalty failed. The darkest hour was yet to come.

So far, we've been focusing on the answer to the question "If God is in control, why is there so much evil in the world?" *Three rebellions*—that's the reason.

It's vital to remember that what has been transpiring up to this point and even into our day is "spiritual warfare" between Yahweh (God) and His adversaries in the spiritual realm and Yahweh and His adversaries here on earth. In the next chapter we will see God's good news answer for us to these 3 rebellions.

Question #5

DOES GOD HAVE AN ANSWER TO ALL 3 REBELLIONS?

God's solution to the problems that arose from these rebellions was radical. He chose to become a man—to join the human race. This is where Jesus enters the story. Jesus was God become man. How do we know that? Here's where you can read about it from the Bible that confirms this wonderful truth. The place we can find out about God, that is reliable and trustworthy, titled "The Supremacy of Christ"

> *"He (The Son) is the image of the invisible God, the firstborn over all creation. For by him all things were created: things in heaven and on earth, visible and invisible, whether thrones or powers or rulers or authorities; all things were created by him and for him. He is before all things, and in him all things hold together. And he is the head of the body, the church; he is the beginning and the firstborn from among the dead, so that in everything he might have the supremacy. For God was pleased to have all his fullness dwell in him, and through him to reconcile to himself all things, whether things on earth or things in heaven, by making peace through his blood, shed on the cross."*
> Colossians 1:15-20, *NIV*

When I began this book, I had no idea that I would actually be writing this chapter on this most relevant weekend, Easter. How affirming it is to recognize God's hand in the timing. Good Friday, the day Jesus was crucified, and Resurrection Sunday, the day He arose.

You see God came as Jesus, and there's so much more to Jesus than the birth of a baby in a manger.

The death and resurrection of Jesus did three things:

1. It *overturned the effects of what the serpent (Satan) had done* in the Garden of Eden—Rebellion #1
2. It *impeded the wickedness* that permeated the world after the Genesis 6—Rebellion #2 by the sons of God.
3. It *took away the authority* of the other defiant gods of the Gentile nations as they rebelled against Yahweh and led these nations to bow to them, as god. Rebellion #3

So, let's unpack how Jesus and His sacrifice worked in each of these Rebellions:

First—you will surely remember that once Satan led Adam and Eve into sin, the result was death. Only Jesus, Who had no sin, dying on behalf of all humanity could reverse the curse of death upon humanity. Only the death of a sinless man would suffice, and that sacrifice fell on the life of Jesus. That meant such a death had to be followed by a resurrection, something only God could accomplish. Again, Jesus was the solution for what happened in Eden. Death, the effect of that first rebellion, was overcome through His resurrection.

There is a familiar verse of Scripture that puts this so clearly:

> *"For God so loved the world, that He gave His only begotten son, that whosoever believeth in Him shall not perish, but have everlasting life."* –John 3:16, KJV

There it is, *"whosoever believeth in Him shall not perish, but have everlasting life."* Death has been conquered and everlasting life is now available to all who believe. Hence, the cancellation of Rebellion #1.

Next, we move to Rebellion #2: Jesus, after His resurrection, shared with His followers that He had to return to the Father's side. Why? Because as he said,

> *"Unless I go away, the Counselor (the Holy Spirit) will not come to you, but if I go, I will send Him to you." –John 16:7, NIV*

My friends, it was the Spirit Who would provide victory over depravity. Paul puts it this way in Galatians 5:16 (NIV),

> *"live by the Spirit and you will not gratify the desires of the sinful nature."*

You see, that's what everyone born inherited from Adam and Eve, a sinful nature, but once we believe in Christ and what He did for us and ask Him into our hearts, the Holy Spirit becomes our Protector. We are no longer helpless against depravity.

It's important to realize, however, that although the powers of darkness have been dethroned, they have not surrendered as we hear in 1 Peter 5:8,

> *"Be self-controlled and alert. Your enemy the devil prowls around like a roaring lion looking for someone to devour."*

But we are reassured in Colossians 1:13 that every person who embraces the salvation offered by God through Jesus is

> *"rescued…from the dominion of darkness and brought… into the Kingdom of the Son He loves."*

Once again, mankind is given freedom of choice: death or eternal life, ongoing slavery and depravity or freedom in Christ.

Rebellion #3 that happened at the Tower of Babel by the sons of God, those supernatural beings, who defected from serving God and became corrupt, abusing the people under their dominion as we can read about in

> *Psalm 82: 1-7, "God presides in the great assembly; he gives judgment among the "gods": How long will you defend the unjust and show partiality to the wicked? Defend the cause of the weak and fatherless; maintain the rights of the poor and oppressed. Rescue the weak and needy; deliver them from the hand of the wicked. They know nothing, they understand nothing. They walk about in darkness; all the foundations of the earth are shaken. I said, 'You are "gods"; you are all sons of the Most High. But you will die like mere men; you will fall like every other ruler.'"*

Let us not forget that God had supernaturally intervened to enable Abraham to have a son, the beginning of the nation of Israel and the promise that one of Abraham's descendants would bless all the nations who God had appeared to have forgotten. Jesus was that descendant as is spelled out in Matthew 1:1-16 under the title, *The Genealogy of Jesus.* Just as an aside here—never skip over passages that might just seem like a meaningless list of names. I remember the very first passage in the Bible my husband read was Matthew 1 and how he ultimately became a believer from reading the "whole Word of God."

Jesus was the promised offspring who would release the Gentiles from those other gods so they could rejoin God's family. In fact, the Spirit's arrival launched an infiltration campaign against the sons of God who had become corrupt. Jesus is the true Hero of the story of redemption.

We see in Acts 2:1-4 that the Spirit arrives in a blaze of glory at Pentecost. At this event, the Spirit enabled the followers of Jesus to speak in all sorts of languages, leading all those who heard to believe in is His death and resurrection. These Jews were descendants of Old Testament Israelites who had been scattered in foreign lands but had gathered for this momentous occasion. From this event they returned to their lands sharing this good news message: Messiah had come, been killed, had risen from the dead, and everyone needed to believe. The promise made to Abraham was being fulfilled!

A very important part of this event was that God was launching a spiritual war to reclaim not only Jews who had rejected Jesus but also Gentiles, the people from the nations He had rejected back at the Tower of Babel.

God was in pursuit of His family, and it didn't matter where His children lived. He wanted them and would find them.

So, my friends, those 3 rebellions that caused so much evil in our world have been disarmed, and we are freed from those events, IF we so choose.

- We have the promise of eternal life.
- We have the power of the Holy Spirit to say no to the depravity that began in Genesis chapter 6.
- We as believers, whether Jew or Gentile, have the blessing of being welcomed into God's Human family. Why? Because of Jesus birth, death and resurrection and the amazing love, grace and mercy of our Father in Heaven.

I remember 30 years ago on Good Friday I believed in Christ as my Saviour and entered into the family of God. May this day be a Day of Reconciliation for you as well.

CHALLENGING QUESTIONS FOR TODAY

Question #6

WHERE DO RELIGIONS COME FROM AND WHY SHOULD WE TRUST CHRISTIANITY OVER OTHERS?

Here we are again, looking at a question that you may have asked yourself, especially in light of the chaos the world is facing during this time. My goal is to help you see the answer as *good news.* Hence, the name of this book—*Questions, Answers, and Good News.*

So, where do religions come from and why should we trust Christianity over other religions?

Let's begin with a definition of the word "Religion." Google, gave me this wording which is simple yet inclusive. "Religion is the belief in a god or in a group of gods: an organized system of beliefs, ceremonies, and rules used to worship a god or a group of gods."[5]

As you may remember, in our first and second chapters, I answered the questions *"Is anyone in control?"* and if there is *"Where can I go to find out about Him that is reliable and trustworthy?"* The answers to these 2 questions, are, God, the Creator of the universe is in control, and we *can* find out about Him, in the Bible. So based on these answers, God (Yahweh) is the one and only true God, and as before we go to the Bible to find out about Him and other religions.

We can also see, as we looked at the answer to why there is so much evil in our world, that from the very beginning in the Garden, a spiritual battle began between God and fallen angels, or as they are often referred

5 Collinsdictionary.com/dictionary/English/religion

to as sons of God led by Satan. This spiritual warfare, my friends, has not ended, hence, we can see the progression of false religions throughout the Old and New Testaments.

There are many false gods mentioned in the Old Testament who were worshipped by the people of Canaan and the nations surrounding the Promised Land. We see in Deuteronomy 32:17 that

> *'they sacrificed to demons, which are not God—gods they had not known."*

or example, when Moses confronted Pharaoh, the Egyptian magicians were able to duplicate some of his miracles, such as turning their staffs into snakes and turning the Nile River into blood. This was warfare, between Yahweh and the false gods of that day. The Good news is, Yahweh was the victor.

I'll mention a few of the major false gods of the Old Testament to help you see how prolific these false religions actually were.

- **Ashtoreth**—the goddess of the Canaanites who was sometimes called a consort or companion of Baal. Note that King Solomon, a Jewish King, who was influenced by his foreign wives, fell into Ashtoreth worship which ultimately led to his downfall (Judges 10:6).

- **Baal**—considered to be the supreme god among the Canaanites was worshiped in many forms, but often as a sun god or storm god. Rites involved with Baal worship included cult prostitution and sometimes human sacrifice. Worshiping Baal was a recurring temptation for the Israelites, which infuriated God the Father, who often punished Israel for their unfaithfulness to him. A famous showdown occurred between the prophets of Baal and Elijah at Mount Carmel. Again, Baal lost this showdown (1 Kings 18).

- **Chemosh**—the national god of the Moabites and the Ammonites. Rites involving this god were said to be cruel and may have involved human sacrifice. Solomon erected an altar to this god found in 2 Kings 23:13 (NIV),

  "This King (King Josiah) also desecrated the high places that were east of Jerusalem on the south of the Hill of Corruption – the ones Solomon, King of Israel, had built for Ashtoreth the vile goddess of the Sidonians, for Chemosh the vile god of Moab and for Molech the detestable god of the people of Ammon."

- **Dagon – the god of the Philistines** was a god of water and grain. Matter of fact Samson, the Hebrew judge, met his death at the temple of Dagon. An amazing battle between Dagon and the true God is found in (1 Samuel 5: 1-5),"

  After the Philistines had captured the ark of God, they took it from Ebenezer to Ashdod. Then they carried the ark into Dagon's temple and set it beside Dagon. When the people of Ashdod rose early the next day, there was Dagon, fallen on his face on the ground before the ark of the LORD! They took Dagon and put him back in his place. But the following morning when they rose, there was Dagon, fallen on his face on the ground before the ark of the LORD! His head and hands had been broken off and were lying on the threshold; only his body remained. That is why to this day neither the priests of Dagon nor any others who enter Dagon's temple at Ashdod step on the threshold."

- **Ancient Egypt had more than 40 false gods**—including: Re, creator sun god; Isis, goddess of magic; Osiris, lord of the afterlife; Thoth, god of worship and the moon and Horus, god of the sun. The 10 plagues of God against Egypt were humiliations of 10 specific Egyptian gods

- **Marduk**—the god of the Babylonians was associated with fertility and vegetation. Important to note is that Marduk actually had 50 names, including Bel and was also worshiped by the Assyrians and Persians (Jeremiah 50:2).

- **Milcom**—also called Malcham, or Molech, the national god of the Ammonites was associated with divination, seeking knowledge of the future through occult means, strongly forbidden by God (Zephaniah 1:5).

Although this is not an exhaustive list of the false gods of the Old Testament, I think you can get the picture.

Looking back over the last 4 chapters at the 3 Rebellions of some of God's spiritual family, we see that these other gods were created as angels but apostatised, meaning they became fallen angels, and then they masqueraded as the true God. That, my friends, is the origin of false religions around the world—then and now.

Another common question is, "If we sincerely worship the god of any religion, are we worshiping the one true God?" The answer is *no.* Other gods are competitors, they are enemies, they are false & demonic. They are not the true God. God made it very clear numerous times in the Old Testament that there were other gods. There were other religions, and His people were not to assume that these gods are manifestations of His own true being, as if God were behind every religion. They are different. They are contenders for deity. They are supernatural, demonic realities.

Hence the first commandment, "You shall have no other gods before me." This is the most crucial issue in our day, ever since Jesus came into the world as the final, decisive revelation of the true God. The true Jesus of history, revealed in Scripture, is the Litmus Test of every claim to supernatural reality. Any religion that does not embrace and worship and obey Jesus as He is revealed in the Bible is a *false religion.* Jesus put it this way in John 5:23 (KJV),

> *"Whoever does not honor the Son does not honor the Father who sent Him."*

No matter what the Pharisees who said they really trusted and believed in the God of the Old Testament said about God, Jesus shows them that they don't love God because they didn't accept Him." Later in John 8:42 we read

> *"If God were your Father, you would love me, for I came from God and I am here."* In 1 John 2:23 *John also says, "No one who denies the Son has the Father, whoever acknowledges the Son has the Father also."*

My conclusion from the Bible is that yes there are real supernatural beings behind other religions, but they are not (Yahweh) the true God. They are contenders against God. They are demons and deceivers and the way to test all claims to truth of a religion is Jesus Christ. He is the final and decisive revelation of the one true God.

So, perhaps it's important that I also provide some insight into other religions of our day. Please note that each of these religions has sects with differing beliefs. The description given here focuses on the core beliefs of each.

HINDUISM

Most Hindus worship one being of ultimate oneness, Brahman, through infinite representations of gods and goddesses. These various deities become incarnate within idols, temples, gurus, rivers, animals, etc. Followers believe their position in this present life was determined by their actions in a previous life. A Hindu's goal is to become free from the law of karma, to be free from continuous reincarnations.

BUDDHISM

Buddhists do not worship any gods or God. The Buddha (Siddhartha Gautama) never claimed to be divine, but rather he is viewed by Buddhists as having attained what they are striving to attain, spiritual enlightenment and with it, freedom from the continuous cycle of life and death. They believe a person has countless rebirths. They also believe that through practiced meditation, a person may reach Nirvana, "the blowing out" of the flame of desire.

ISLAM

Muslims, believe there is the one almighty God named Allah who is infinitely superior to and transcendent from humankind. They believe He is a powerful and strict judge who will be merciful toward followers depending on the sufficiency of their life's good works and religious devotion. Though a Muslim honors several prophets, Muhammad is considered the last prophet and his words and lifestyle are the authority that they must follow. That lifestyle includes 5 religious duties and based on one's faithfulness to these duties, a Muslim hopes to enter Paradise. If not, they will be eternally punished in hell.

For many people, Islam matches their expectations about religion and deity. Islam teaches that there is one supreme deity, who is worshiped through good deeds and disciplined religious rituals.

NEW AGE

New Age spirituality promotes the development of the person's own power or divinity, which is described as a higher consciousness within themselves. A person pursuing spiritual development would see themselves as deity, the cosmos, or the universe. It actually acknowledges many gods and goddesses, as in Hinduism. New Age teaches eastern mysticism and spiritual metaphysical and psychic techniques, such as breathing exercises, chanting, drumming and transcendental meditation to develop an altered consciousness and ones' own divinity.

JUDAISM

Judaism is an ethnic religion comprising the collective, religious, cultural, legal tradition, and civilization of the Jewish people. Judaism is considered by religious Jews to be the expression of the covenant God established with the Children of Israel. It encompasses a wide body of texts, practices, theological positions, and forms of organization. The Torah is part of the larger text known as the Tanakh or the Hebrew Bible, with supplemental, oral tradition represented by later texts such as the Midrash and the Talmud. Their faith in Scripture ends with the Old Testament, hence, Jesus is not a part of their belief system.

CHRISTIANITY

Christians believe in one, eternal God, Creator of all that is. He is viewed as a loving God, Who offers everyone a personal relationship with Himself.

In His life on Earth, Jesus Christ did not identify Himself as a prophet pointing to God or as a teacher of enlightenment. Rather, Jesus claimed to be *God in human form.* He performed miracles, healed the sick, brought people back to life, forgave people of their sin and said that anyone who believed in Him would have eternal life.

Followers of Jesus regard the Bible as God's written message to humankind. In addition to being an historical record of Jesus' life and miracles, the Bible reveals His personality, His love and truth, and how one can know and relate to God as a friend.

Christians believe that all people sin. They see Jesus as their Savior, as the Messiah who was prophesied by all the prophets of the Old Testament in the Bible. They believe that Jesus Christ, out of love for us, paid for the sin of all of humanity by dying on a cross. Three days later, He rose from the dead as He prophesied, proving His deity.

In conclusion, let's see how distinct these religions are:

- Hindus acknowledge multitudes of gods and goddesses.
- Buddhists say there is no deity.
- Muslins believe in a powerful but unknowable God – reachable only by good deeds and practices.
- New Age Spiritualists believe they are God.
- Jewish people believe in Yahweh God but reject the New Testament. They are still waiting for their Messiah.
- Christians believe in a loving God Who created us to know Him and Who came as Jesus Christ to set us free from our sin and open the door to eternal life.

I've given you a lot to think about, but the false gods of our day and in the time before Christ, are always working to lead the world away from the One Who claimed to be in John 14:6, *"the way, the truth and the life."* I could go on to discuss the cults that have arisen in our day, but I hope you will recognize their false claims considering this truth found in Acts 4:12 (NIV),

> *"Salvation is found in no one else, for there is no other name under heaven given to men by which we must be saved."*

My Friends, I truly believe this is *good news* to understand and believe in a Savior, even in a world that seems to be upside down.

In the next Chapter, we will move along to looking at the question, *"How do we find peace in this world of chaos?"*

Question #7

HOW DO I FIND PEACE IN THIS WORLD OF CHAOS?

I believe many of us have been asking ourselves this question during this time of turmoil.

Let's begin by considering what I mean when I say "peace." There are two types of peace, internal and external. We often hear the term as it would relate to external, "How I yearn for some *peace* and quiet." I'm sure we who have children might have often voiced this desire. We also hear calls for peace like this: "I sure hope we will see our world governments refrain from war and embrace *peace* during this time of trouble."

Although these are worthy desires, they are not what I want to talk about in this chapter. Instead, we will focus on the concept of "internal peace" or as it's often referred to, "inner peace."

Over the last 18 months, I've heard many reports that there has been an explosion of calls to suicide hotlines all over the country. I would say this is no surprise. People are dealing with financial stress, social isolation, health concerns, and 24/7 news outlets telling us how bad things are and how bad they still may become.

I don't know about you, but I've had a variety of storms in my life, and with the hope of finding "inner peace," I ventured into some very scary and dangerous places. Society tells us we can find answers and peace by blocking out the problems with the use of drugs or alcohol. Or that we can just turn off the news where our minds and emotions are dulled, therefore the fear and the pain seem to go away, at least for a little while.

The problem is that it comes back, usually worse than before. Why? Because there is no *peace* in these medications.

Maybe the answer lies in checking out 'new age' meditations, like we talked about in Chapter Six. I remember specifically trying to find peace in a transcendental meditation gathering where I was encouraged to empty my mind, hum, and escape the turmoil in my life. I'm so grateful that I was protected during these sessions and the devil didn't get his way.

We might be encouraged to check out our horoscopes to see "what the stars have in mind for our lives." Again, we must remember that this dependence upon astrology is led by Satan, the enemy of God and man.

So, is inner peace possible? Maybe we just need to hunker down and keep our minds off the problems we hear about 24/7, such as lives being lost, economies crashing, masks, social distancing, and isolation. What's really frightening is how people are coping. Here's a few statistics that reinforce what I've been talking about.

What commodities are flourishing? Well, that would be liquor and beer, cannabis, online gambling, and pornography. I would suggest people are trying to cope, but I'd also suggest these coping mechanisms don't work. They merely add to the problem.

Let's consider ways we can find "peace in the midst of the storm" by looking at 4 examples of people caught up in terrible situations and how they found peace of mind.

Joni Earickson Tada has an amazing story to tell. She is an author, speaker and international advocate for people with disabilities. At age 17, she became a paraplegic from a diving accident and has since then been wheelchair bound. But that hasn't stopped her from finding peace even though she's also had to go through two bouts of cancer. I was privileged to hear her speak at a special conference in Atlanta, Georgia in 2000 and was amazed at her ability to actually look at her situation and be able to says things like:

> *"He has chosen not to heal me, but to hold me. The more intense the pain, the closer His embrace. Heartache forces us to embrace God out of desperate urgent need. God is never closer than when your heart is aching."*[6]

Thank You Joni, for helping us to perhaps put things going on in our lives today into perspective.

Fanny Crosby was blinded as a young child, but that didn't stop her from writing 9,000 songs, many of which bring hope and peace to those who hear them. Here is one verse and chorus from one of Fanny's songs:[7]

> *"I must have the Saviour with me.*
> *In the onward march of life;*
> *Through the tempest and the sunshine,*
> *Through the battle and the strife.*
> *"Then my soul shall fear no ill.*
> *Let him lead me where he will.*
> *I will go without a murmur,*
> *And his footsteps follow still.*

Fanny Crosby and Joni Earickson Tada knew what it was like to deal with trial and tribulations in their lives, but they also knew where to find peace.

In 1873, Horatio Gates Spafford's wife and four daughters were traveling to Europe on an ocean liner when they were in a terrible collision and all four children drowned. As he was travelling on another ship to meet up with his wife, the captain of the ship stopped where his daughters were lost at sea, and he wrote these words to the song *It Is Well with My Soul.*

---

6 www.goodrads.com quote from "A Place of Healing" by Joni Eareckson Toda

7 http://hymnary.org written by Fanny Crosby

"When peace like a river attendeth my way,
When sorrows like sea billows roll,
What ever my lot, thou hast taught me to say,
It is well, It is well with my soul."[8]

Imagine finding this kind of peace in such a terrible time.

Lastly, I'd like to share another story of a Salvation Army Officer, Stanley Ditmer, who found peace during a time of hardship and trying times and penned the words of this song, *I'm In His Hands*:

"I shall not fear though darkened clouds may gather round me;
The God I serve is one who cares and understands.
Although the storms I face, would threaten to confound me,
Of this I am assured: I'm in his hands.
I'm in his hands, I'm in his hands;
Whate're the future holds I'm in his hands,
The days I cannot see
Have all been planned for me:
His way is best you see;
I'm in his hands."

This song in particular rings very true to me. 25 years ago, as I was laying on a stretcher awaiting surgery and was feeling somewhat alone and fearful, I prayed that God would look after me and the words to this song came to me, loud and clear, I'm in his hands. Oh, what peace the Savior gives!

Going into God's Word, let me leave you with the assurance that you too can find Peace in the midst of this storm we're living through:

"The Lord is a refuge for the oppressed, a stronghold in times of trouble." –Psalm 9:9

---

[8] http://hymnary.org/text written by Horatio Gates Spafford 1873

> *"I will lie down and sleep in peace for you alone O Lord, make me dwell in safety."–Psalm 4:8*

> *"God is our refuge and strength, an ever-present help in trouble." –Psalm 46:1*

Here is a promise that Jesus gave to His followers who were in great fear of what was ahead of them,

> *"Peace I leave with you, my peace I give you. I do not give as the world gives. Do not let your hearts be troubled and do not be afraid." –John 14:26*

That my friends is a wonderful promise that we can claim during this time of trouble. God is in control and through Jesus we can rest in the truth that trusting in Him as our Savior will bring us this "inner peace" that those we've looked at today found.

Question #8

DO HEAVEN AND HELL EXIST?

This is a troubling question as we contemplate what may lie ahead.

I hope you will see this answer as good_news even in a subject we don't often like to talk about. Benjamin Franklin wrote in a letter to Jean-Baptiste Leroy that, "Nothing can be said to be certain except death and taxes."[9]

We all pay taxes, and if we don't, there are penalties. But what about the first part—death? Do you know of someone over the age of 150 who hasn't died? No, so that statement is correct.

As we look around us at the chaos in our world due to this pandemic, we see the eruption of protests and riots breaking out all over the world—with deadly consequences in many cases. I've noticed there are more and more people picking up Bibles, maybe for the first time, and more people tuning to YouTube preachers for answers! Why? Because *fear grips the soul* when there seems to be something going on around us that we can't control—something that might ultimately lead to our "early physical death".

My husband and I were pastors for almost 8 years in a Midwest city. We connected with a wonderful group of people who were a complete opposite of church folk. Every week we joined them in a friendly game of darts at the local Royal Canadian Legion Hall. They all knew we were pastors, yet they welcomed us with open arms. There was one man

---

9 Madesen Pririe, "Death and Taxes," Adam Smith Institute, November 13, 2019, https://www.adamsmith.org/blog/death-and-taxes

who had come from the world of bikers. He made it clear to us from the very beginning that he didn't want us preaching to him. We honored his request and for the next few years, we became his Friday night friends.

One day about 6 years into our friendship, we received a call asking if he could come to our church to talk to us. He'd just had an appointment with his doctor and was told he had an inoperable malignant brain tumor and had a relatively short time to live.

He realized death was at the door. He told us about his diagnosis and then said, "I'm not sure what lies ahead for me, but even though I don't know much about God, I do believe there is a heaven and because of that I also believe there is a hell, and I don't want to end up there. I've watched you folks over these last few years, and I trust that you will help me prepare, that you will show me how I can be sure I don't go to hell, and that I will leave this world and go to heaven." What an honor that was!

We explained to him the truth of Salvation and then gave him a Bible and a list of sections he should begin reading and then we made appointments to help him with any questions he had, and to ultimately prepare his soul to meet God. He made the choice to accept the Lord Jesus as his Savior. At his funeral, we were able to say with assurance that he was in Heaven.

I share that story to help you see that as we face the questions and challenges of our world today, there is a heaven and a hell. Most importantly there is a way to be sure where you will spend eternity.

As we discovered in chapter 2 of this journey, there is a place we can go to find reliable and trustworthy answers to the big and small questions we face every day—the Bible.

My goal today is not to provide you with all the details of either heaven or hell, but to share with you Scripture passages that I hope will open your eyes and heart to believe they exist and why it's so important we consider our destiny.

First, we'll look at heaven. Now the Old Testament doesn't say a great deal compared to the New Testament about heaven, but what it does say is powerful. Here are a few relevant passages.

> *"Therefore hear the word of the LORD: I saw the LORD sitting on his throne with all the multitude of heaven standing around him on his right and on his left." –1 Kings 22:19, NIV*

This verse speaks of God revealing Himself in a prophetic revelation, as "a king enthroned in heaven" surrounded by angels (the sons of God, His spiritual family) who do His bidding.

> *"The LORD looks down from heaven on the sons of men to see if there are any who understand, any who seek God."* –Psalm 14:2

> *"The LORD is good to those whose hope is in him, to the one who seeks him."* –Lamentations 3:25

God is in heaven, yet all we have to do is seek Him and He will be found.

We also see historical and prophetical writers such as Nehemiah and Isaiah declare the truth of a heaven.

> *"I answered them by saying, 'The God of heaven will give us success'"* (Nehemiah 2:20, NIV). *"This is what the LORD says; 'Heaven is my throne, and the earth is my footstool'"* (Isaiah 66:1, NIV).

They knew where their help came from. In the book of Job, we hear God reprimanding Job and his friends for questioning Him. He reminds them that

"Everything under heaven belongs to me" (Job 41:11, NIV).

Here are a few more verses from the Psalms that attest to the existence of Heaven as the dwelling place of God and His spiritual family, the angels or the holy ones.

> *"From heaven the LORD looks down and sees all mankind; from His dwelling place he watches all who live on earth." –Psalm 33:13-14, NIV*

> *"The LORD has established his throne in heaven, and his kingdom rules over all. Praise the LORD, you his angels, you mighty ones who do his bidding, who obey his word. Praise the LORD, all His heavenly hosts, you His servants who do his will…Praise the LORD, O my soul." –Psalm 103:19-22, NIV*

The picture of heaven that seems to be emphasized in the Old Testament is that it is the dwelling place of God. We see through the eyes of the Old Testament writers that God is watching. He is looking to see if there is anyone interested in Him, who seeks Him, who understands His holiness, who is interested in finding a way to Him—a way to heaven—He wants us there with Him for all eternity.

Now, we will look into the New Testament to see what it has to say about heaven.

There is a wonderful explanation found in the book of Revelation chapters 21 and 22 and I would suggest you read it through. I'd like to share with you the opening verse of that section:

> *"Then I saw a new heaven and a new earth" (Revelation 21:1).*

The writer of Revelation, the Apostle John, had been provided with the privilege of being with God in heaven. He was given a wonderful picture of what was to come. The last verse in this section says,

"The Angel said to me, 'These words are trustworthy and true'" (Revelation 22:6).

It has been said that when the precious stones found in the foundation of the New Jerusalem in Revelation 21: 19-21 are placed in the order described in John's vision, they form a perfect harmony of color. And of course, I've always found it amazing to read that there really will be 'pearly gates' and instead of hoarding 'bars of gold' like we do here on earth, the streets we will be walking on it will be paved with it. How amazing will this place be!

Heaven is God's way of having a permanent home for you, in His presence. Heaven is God's gift to all those who seek Him, who choose Him, who acknowledge His authority, His love and His saving grace and turn to His Son, Jesus, as their Savior.

Now we turn to the alternative. This is not an easy subject, but it is necessary to remember that as sure as I am that there is a heaven, I am equally sure *there is a hell.* The Bible actually has more to say about hell than it does about heaven. There is a passage in Luke chapter 16 spoken by Jesus Himself that explains things much better than I ever could. It is entitled "The Rich Man and Lazarus." Some people say this illustration by Jesus is a parable, however, many are inclined to think not. You see if it is, it's the only parable where Jesus gave a name to one of the characters. Let's read it as if Jesus was clearly teaching the listeners—and that would be us—that there is a heaven and a hell.

"There was a rich man who was dressed in purple and fine linen and lived in luxury every day. At his gate was laid a beggar named Lazarus, covered with sores and longing to eat what fell from the rich man's table. Even the dogs came and licked his sores.

The time came when the beggar died and the angels carried him to Abraham's side. The rich man also died and was buried. In Hades, where he was in torment, he looked up and saw Abraham far away, with Lazarus by his side. So he called to him. 'Father Abraham, have pity on me and send Lazarus to dip the tip of his finger in water and cool my tongue, because I am in agony in this fire.'

But Abraham replied, 'Son, remember that in your lifetime you received your good things, while Lazarus received bad things, but now he is comforted here and you are in agony. And besides all this, between us and you a great chasm has been set in place, so that those who want to go from here to you cannot, nor can anyone cross over from there to us.

He answered, 'Then I beg you, father, send Lazarus to my family, for I have five brothers. Let him warn them, so that they will not also come to this place of torment.'

Abraham replied. 'They have Moses and the Prophets; let them listen to them.'

'No, father Abraham', he said, 'but if someone from the dead goes to them, they will repent.'

He said to him, 'If they do not listen to Moses and the Prophets, they will not be convinced even if someone rises from the dead.'

–Luke 16:19-31

That last verse is actually prophetic. Jesus is teaching that if a person's mind is closed and Scripture is rejected, no evidence—even Jesus' resurrection doesn't convince people.

What I hope from this lesson is that you will agree that heaven and hell are real places. That the teaching of the One Who was resurrected, Jesus the Christ, will stir your heart as you contemplate what might be coming next in our world, our country and our communities. That like our friend I spoke about earlier in the opening of this chapter, you will reach out to someone you trust, and make sure you're ready to meet God. That you will remember the truth in John 3:16,

> *"For God so loved the world that He gave His only begotten son, that whosoever believeth in Him shall not perish but have eternal life."*

Remember my friends, the *life* He speaks of in this verse is life with Him in Heaven.

I have often heard people respond to this teaching with the comment, "I don't believe there is a hell." My friends, remember the rich man. He didn't believe in a hell before he arrived there either! God wants us to be prepared, to open our hearts to the truth. This may be your day to believe and to have a place reserved for you in *Heaven!*

Question #9

WHAT DO WE KNOW ABOUT ANGELS?

In this chapter, we'll begin a 3-part miniseries looking at what the Bible has to say about angels, demons and lastly spiritual warfare and how these fit into what's happening in our world today.

There is so much most people don't know about the Spiritual Realm—the place where God's spiritual family resides. When we looked at the question "If God is in Control, why is there so much evil in our world?" we saw that God created two families—His spiritual family and His human family. Hence the terms, "human beings" and "spiritual beings" of which angels are a part.

So now we will be looking at members of the heavenly host who are by nature *unembodied* spirit beings. Their normal domain is the spiritual world. They were present with God before the creation of the world and human beings. You may wonder if the members of the heavenly host are eternal, the answer is *no.* There is only one Spirit Being who is eternal, meaning that He had no beginning and no end, is never described as being created, and whose existence preceded creation.

Psalm 90:2 says,

> *"Before the mountains were born or you brought forth the whole world, from everlasting to everlasting you are God."*

All other Elohim were created by the lone, uncreated God of the Bible.

Let's consider for a moment that if we desire to know what the members of the heavenly host are like, we should consider ourselves as similar. Psalm 8:5 (ESV), a passage that informs us that God has made us *"a little lower than the heavenly beings (Elohim)."*

Yet God shared His attributes with us as He first did with them. Remember He created us in "His image." What are members of the heavenly host like? They are like God and like us. Think about these attributes that we share with our Creator: intelligence, creativity, emotions, rationality, and volition. Our fellow imagers, the members of the heavenly host have them as well, because they are also His imagers.

Our embodiment naturally means we live with significant limitations that unembodied intelligent beings don't. Because of what happened in Eden, our lifespans are severely curtailed. We die after a brief existence in the world God made for us. It is only at that point that we experience the presence of God presuming we are part of His family through redemptive grace.

We are thus far less intelligent, creative, and wise than the members of the spiritual world. We simply do not know what they have learned through access to God and lifespans of many eons. They even have the attribute of free will, which we saw when they chose to exercise a revolt to God. However, according to God's word there are still thousands who remain loyal.

So now let's consider these spiritual beings by name and purpose which include angels, cherubim, seraphim and archangels.

It's important to note that the terms angel, cherubim and seraphim are not interchangeable. They are, in effect, job descriptions performed by different spirit beings. In biblical literature, cherubim and seraphim are never sent to people to deliver messages. That task belongs to angels. Cherubim and seraphim are heavenly throne guardians, a role that at times brings them into contact with humans, but they are not sent to earth to instruct people.

We also see that whenever angels encounter humans in their messaging role, they appear in human form. In the Old Testament their appearance makes them indistinguishable from men. It is only when they do something unearthly that their transcendent nature becomes apparent. The only visible exceptions in this pattern are found in the New Testament where members of the heavenly host appear to people along with luminous glory as we see in Luke 2: 9,

> *"An angel of the Lord appeared to them, and the glory of the Lord shone around them."* Also in Matthew 28:3, *"His appearance was like lightning, and his clothes were white as snow."*

It's also important to note that opposite to popular belief, angels are never described as having inhuman features such as wings or multiple faces. This helps us conclude that angels, those divine beings sent to earth to interact with people, look like people and are always referred to as male although as spirit beings they are genderless. The flesh they assume is gendered (male) because it is flesh.

When it comes to affecting the material world, we can see that they assume material form and act upon material objects. For instance, the two angels in Genesis 19:11 who visited Lot, were able to strike the men of Sodom (both young and old) with blindness

> *"Then they struck the men who were at the door of the house, young and old, with blindness so that they could not find the door."*

They were the cause of that effect.

We also see that an angel somehow freed Peter from his shackles as they opened an iron gate without touching it in Acts 12:10,

> *"They passed the first and second guards and came to the iron gate leading to the city, it opened for them by itself, and they went through it. When they had walked the length of one street, suddenly the angel left him."*

They also struck Herod with a disease in Acts 12:23,

> *"Immediately, because Herod did not give praise to God, an angel of the Lord struck him down."*

We also see that angels moved the stone from the tomb of Jesus Matthew 28:2,

> *"There was a violent earthquake for an angel of the Lord came down from heaven and, going to the tomb, rolled back the stone and sat on it."*

Now let's look at those we might consider "Important Angels."

First—The Angel of Yahweh (the Angel of the LORD)

In the Old Testament this is the most well-known angel and is Yahweh Himself in the visible form of a man. Exodus 23:20-22 says,

> *"See I am sending an angel ahead of you to guard you along the way and to bring you to the place I have prepared. Pay attention to him and listen to what he says.... If you listen carefully to what he says and do all that I say. I will be an enemy to your enemies and will oppose those who oppose you. My angel will go ahead of you and bring you into the land...I will wipe [your enemies] out."*

God describes the angel as having His name in him, He is telling Moses that His very presence is within this angel. The angel is the visible form of Yahweh Himself.

In Judges 2:1 we read this angel of Yahweh reported that he accomplished the mission: *"Now the angel of the LORD...said, 'I brought you up from Egypt and brought you into the land that I swore to give to your ancestors.'"* There are other references you may like to look up that refer to this angel, Deuteronomy 6:10-11, 7:1, 9:4, 11:23; Ezekiel 20:28 as well as in

Genesis 1:11-13 when Jacob sees him standing in Bethel in the house of God.

Second—The Commander of Yahweh's Army

Another significant member of the heavenly host is the unnamed commander of Yahweh's heavenly host, His army who appeared to Joshua on the cusp of a conquest found in Joshua 5:13-15,

> *"Now when Joshua was near Jericho, he looked up and saw a man standing in front of him with a drawn sword in his hand. Joshua went up to him and asked, 'Are you for us for our enemies?' 'Neither,' he replied, 'but as commander of the army of the LORD, I have now come.' Then Joshua fell facedown to the ground in reverence, and asked him, 'What message does my Lord have for his servant?' The commander of the LORD'S army replied, 'Take off your sandals for the place where you are standing is Holy.' And Joshua did so.'"*

Following along with the reference to "*Take off your sandals from your feet for the place you are standing is holy*" we are taken back to another passage and the burning bush incident in *Exodus 3:5, "Do not come any closer,' God said. 'Take off your sandals, for the place where you are standing is holy ground.'"* It's important to note that the angel of Yahweh was in the burning bush passage. We hear Stephen make reference to this truth in Acts 7:30-31 where he notes that an angel *"appeared to Moses in the flames of a burning bush in the desert near Mount Sinai. When he saw this, he was amazed at the sight. As he went over to look more closely, he heard the Lord's voice."*

There are also several passages in the Old Testament that describe an end-times conflict involving the army of the holy ones, unleashing the wrath of God on both His earthly and heavenly enemies. If you read a description of this wrath in (Zechariah 14) you will see in verse 5 a reference to this group of angels

> *"You will flee by my mountain valley, for it will extend to Azal. You will flee as you fled from the earthquake in the days of Uzziah king of Judah. Then the LORD my God will come, and all the holy ones with Him."*

We can also find in sections of the Qumran scrolls that God's army during this time consisted of "a multitude of holy ones" and "hosts of angels" in heaven and "the elect ones of the holy nation" on earth. Both groups are to be mustered for the battle (1 QM 15:13-14). This picture is also present in other second temple literary works such as 2 Maccabees.

Third—The Archangels

Gabriel and Michael are best discussed together since their appearances are in the same chapters of the book of (Daniel chapters 8 -12) in the following verses:

> *"And I heard a man's voice from the Ulai calling, "Gabriel, tell this man the meaning of the vision." – 8:16*
>
> *"While I was still in prayer, Gabriel, the man I had seen in the earlier vision, came to me in swift flight about the time of the evening sacrifice." –9:21*
>
> In *10:5-6* we see a description of Gabriel, *"I looked up and there before me was a man dressed in linen, with a belt of the finest gold around his waist. His body was like chrysolite, his face like lightning, his eyes like flaming torches, his arms and legs like the gleam of burnished bronze, and his voice like the sound of a multitude."*
>
> *"But the prince of the Persian kingdom resisted me (Gabriel) twenty-one days. Then Michael, one of the chief princes,*

came to help me, because I was detained there with the king of Persia."–10:13

"At that time Michael, the great prince who protects your people, will arise. There will be a time of distress such as has not happened from the beginning of nations until then" (12:1).

Along with these two, an unidentified "Prince of the host" appears.

Gabriel and Michael are the lone angels mentioned by name in the Bible and are well known as archangels. You see this term used of Michael in the New Testament *Jude 9,*

"But even the archangel Michael when he was disputing with the devil about the body of Moses, did not dare to bring a slanderous accusation against Him, but said "The Lord rebuke you!"

You can also find examples of archangels in the book of 1 Enoch as "over angels," and they seem to be busily in charge of maintaining created order, plotting out times and seasons and praising the Most High.

For New Testament authors, "angelos" is a catchall term for the supernatural agents who faithfully attend God. Again, we only see two angels named Michael and Gabriel. There is not a lot of emphasis given in the New Testament to archangels except in 1 Thessalonians 4:16,

"For the Lord himself will come down from heaven, with a loud command, with the voice of the archangel and with the trumpet call of God."

Here they proclaim the return of Christ although this angel is not named.

There is a very important passage found in Ephesians and Colossians where Paul refers to the supernatural beings appointed by God over the nations as rulers, thrones, dominions and authorities hostile to God.

We will look more closely at this passage when we delve into part three of this series dealing with spiritual warfare.

If I can leave you with one important truth from this teaching, it is that there are a variety of spiritual beings created by God deemed His first family, who we will one day be a part of. Matter of fact, Paul tells us in 1 Corinthians 6:3 that we will actually *"judge angels."* We as *'sons of God'* through Christ will join with the sons of God who already serve God in His Divine Council. Imagine that!

Question #10

WHAT DO WE KNOW ABOUT THE POWERS OF DARKNESS?

Some of what we'll look at follows along with information I've already shared in previous chapters when we looked at the question Why is there so much evil in the world? and What do we know about Angels?

Let's begin by looking at some terms we need to understand about these powers of darkness

We begin with the term Demon(s), which is an evil spirit, a source or agent of evil. They are considered spiritual beings at work behind corrupt human power structures and in the Bible, they also work on a personal level. They are described as animating and exploiting humanity's greed and selfishness as well as the weakness of their mortal bodies.

I find it very interesting that in all 4 gospels we see Jesus healing a variety of illnesses and diseases of which demon-possession was also mentioned. Note that in each of these examples from the gospel of Matthew Jesus drove out the demon(s) from the people afflicted.

> (Matthew 4:24) *"News about him (Jesus) spread all over Syria, and people brought to him all who were ill with various diseases, those suffering severe pain, the demon-possessed, those having seizures and the paralyzed and he healed them."*

> (Matthew 8:16) *"When evening came, many who were demon-possessed were brought to him (Jesus), and he drove out the spirits with a word and healed all the sick."*

(Matthew 8:28) *"When he (Jesus) arrived at the other side in the region of the Gadarenes, two demon-possessed men coming from the tombs met him. They were so violent that no one could pass that way."*

(Matthew 12:22) *"Then they brought him a demon-possessed man who was blind and mute, and Jesus healed him, so that he could both talk and see."*

(Matthew 17:18) *"Jesus rebuked the demon, and it came out of the boy, and he was healed from that moment."*

(Matthew10:8) Jesus sends out the 12 disciples with this instruction *"Heal the sick, raise the dead, cleanse those who have leprosy, drive out demons. Freely you have received, freely give."*

"Satan," or as it's often seen "The Satan," actually stands for "The Adversary" which certainly seems appropriate to his actions. A very interesting question that has come up is this: Was Satan the tempter in Genesis Chapter 3?

Let's do a quick recap: God and His spiritual family were living together in the Garden of Eden along with His new human family. In our discussion about angels, we saw that there were actually three beings who would have been there with God also known as the sons of God (members of his divine council) cherubim, seraphim and angels. Hence, Adam and Eve would have been familiar with these beings.

Later in the book of Isaiah, we find that the Hebrew word for "seraphim" was "snake" therefore, the tempter that led to the fall of humanity or physical death, and the separation of God and His spiritual beings from human beings or spiritual death, being described as a "snake" seems to make perfect sense. We saw how this original rebel was cast down, expelled from God's presence to earth and under the earth in the realm of the dead. Going forward to the fallen sons of God, or watchers as they are known as in Genesis 6:1-4, we see they were likewise imprisoned in the underworld.

Later in the scene at the tower of Babel, the rebellious Elohim (sons of God) who were placed over the nations by God are destined to the same fate, eternal separation from God, although their end will come only at the day of the Lord. Hence. they are still around, working behind the scenes to bring down nations and peoples to keep them from the Lord.

Then we find in the New Testament that the namesake of the rebel of Eden eventually became referred to as Satan. The term "adversary" was a sensible moniker, given the rebel's opposition to God's human imagers and His plan for them.

From this point forward, we'll spend most of our time looking at the influence of these powers of darkness in the New Testament and even in our present day.

The lead villain of the New Testament went by several names, some of which are interpretive, while others have Old Testament roots. Here are a few of those names, many of which you will be familiar:

Tempter—Matthew 4:3 "*The tempter came to him (Jesus) and said, 'If you are the Son of God, tell these stones to become bread'*".

Enemy—Matthew 13:38 "*The field is the world, and the good seed stands for the sons of the kingdom. The weeds are the sons of the evil one. (The enemy)*

Satan—as a proper name occurs 36 times in the New Testament and is interchangeable with the term devil. Revelation 12:9 mentions him three times, "*The great dragon was hurled down – that ancient serpent called the devil, or Satan, who leads the whole world astray.*"

Devil—a title that means slanderer, liar, and father of lies. John 8:44 says, "*You belong to your father, the devil, and you want to carry out your* *father's desire. He was a murderer from the beginning, not holding to the truth, for there is no truth in him. When he lies, he speaks his native language for he is a liar and the father of lies.* We also see in the Gospels the devil is "portrayed as the adversary of Jesus and the enemy of His work—as seen in the temptation of Jesus in the wilderness in Matthew 4: 1-11.

Leader of other evil spirits—Matthew 25:41, *"Then he will say to those on his left. 'Depart from me, you who are cursed, into the eternal fire prepared for the devil and his angels."*

The prince of demons, Beelzebub— Matthew 12:24, *"It is only by Beelzebub, the prince of demons, that this fellow drives out demons?"* Here we see that Matthew considered the minions of Satan's kingdom to be demons.

Prince or Ruler of this world—found three times in the gospel of John in the context where Jesus is referring to his own death and its significance. Here in John 14:30, *"I will not speak with you much longer, for the prince of this world_is coming."*

Our good news today begins with Jesus' victory over Satan's temptation in the wilderness which is ultimately a victory over the gods of the nations that were abandoned by Yahweh at Babel. Let's look at Matthew 4:8-11,

> *"Again, the devil took him to a very high mountain and showed him all the kingdoms of the world and their splendor. 'All this I will give you,' he said, 'if you will bow down and worship me.' Jesus said to him, 'Away from me, Satan! For it is written: 'Worship the Lord your God and serve him only.' Then the devil left him.'"*

It's important to note that this judgment on the nations was never intended to be permanent. Jesus the One promised by Yahweh through the lineage of Abraham and his offspring would bless all the nations with freedom from these rebels.

We can see God's Plan in Genesis 12:3 as He promises Abraham

> *"I will bless those who bless you, and whoever curses you I will curse; and all peoples on earth will be blessed through you."*

Had Jesus failed in the wilderness temptation, that plan would have failed. The reversal and demise of Satan's kingdom has begun for good. From this point forward, linked to what Jesus accomplished on the cross, there will be no kingdom failure. Jesus did ascend after his resurrection, and the Spirit came to empower believers to overcome depravity in Romans 8:2,

> *"Through Christ Jesus the law of the Spirit of life set me free from the law of sin and death"*

and to restore the disinherited nations to the family of God as seem in Acts 2 at Pentecost.

The Good News—the gospel message is that all who are members of the kingdom of Jesus are no longer under the curse of death. By definition, Satan's kingdom no longer has any hold upon them. The devil remains active in the world until the final judgment, blinding the minds of people to prevent them from joining the kingdom of Jesus, but he has no accusation to bring against those who belong to Christ. Scripture describes being in Christ in Revelation 12:10,

> *"For the accuser of our brothers, who accuses them before our God day and night, has been hurled down."*

Christ's resurrection and ascension are the centrepiece of the New Testament and our understanding of the victory over other supernatural rebels.

The book of Acts is nothing less than the liberation of the people of the world held captive by the gods of the nations who enslaved them in their idolatry and unbelief. If you want to see how invasive this captivity of gentile nations was, just take some time and read through the books of Judges and 1st and 2nd Kings. False gods, demons and idol worship was everywhere, leading not only the nations surrounding Israel astray but often Israel herself.

We see Paul reference these gods in 1 Corinthians 10:19-20,

> *"Do I mean then that a sacrifice offered to an idol is anything, or that an idol is anything? No, but the sacrifices of pagans are offered to demons, not to God, and I do not want you to be participants with demons."*

I will delve into Paul's teaching in the book of Ephesians in the next chapter when we focus on "spiritual warfare" which has been going on from the very beginning in the Garden of Eden until today. A couple of other questions you might find interesting that we will look at are:

- Can a Christian be demon possessed?
- What do these powers of darkness fear?
- Will we witness their demise?

Will Satan be destroyed? That one I'll answer right now. Yes—in the book of Revelation.

> *"And I saw an angel coming down out of heaven, having the key to the Abyss and holding in his hand a great chain. He seized the dragon, that ancient serpent, who is the devil, or Satan and bound him for a thousand years. He threw him into the Abyss, and locked and sealed it over him, to keep him from deceiving the nations anymore until the thousand years were ended. After that, he must be set free for a short time."* And then on in (verses 7-10), *"When the thousand years are over, Satan will be released*

> *from his prison and will go out to deceive the nations in the four corners of the earth—Gog and Magog—to gather them for battle. In number they are like the sand on the seashore. They marched across the breadth of the earth and surrounded the camp of God's people, the city he loves. But fire came down from heaven and devoured them. And the devil, who deceived them, was thrown into the lake of burning sulfur, where the beast and the false prophet had been thrown. They will be tormented day and night for ever and ever." –Revelation 20:1-3*

I hope you feel more knowledgeable about the spiritual realm and who resides there, and the truths of the plan God has had all along to deal with these rebels. There is a heavenly host of faithful angels who we will join with one day around the throne of God as we read in Revelation 5:11,

> *"Then I looked and heard the voice of many angels, numbering thousands upon thousands, and ten thousand times ten thousand. They encircled the throne and the living creatures and the elders."*

How wonderful that will be, all because God had a plan and Jesus is a Saviour.

Question #11

WHAT DO WE KNOW ABOUT SPIRITUAL WARFARE?

Here we are in the last part of this miniseries looking at the questions: What do we know about Angels? What do we know about demons and the powers of darkness? And now to the question, what do we know about spiritual warfare?

Let's begin by considering what we know about warfare in general. War starts between enemies and there are usually good guys and bad guys involved. Hence, what we will look at today is the battle between angels and demons and God's heavenly hosts as well as their battle with mankind.

There are battles going on in the heavenly realm and here in our world as well. Battles that we don't see with our eyes.

And they all began when God's spiritual family, who were upset that He had created a new human family and a special place for them, chose to rebel against Him and the war began. We looked at these 3 rebellions in the section titled, Why Is There So Much Evil in the World? It became very clear that God has enemies and these enemies are determined to lead mankind away from God and put themselves in His place—hence bringing about our downfall. Be very aware, Satan and his followers do not care for us, they have only one goal and that is our destruction which means keeping us away from Jesus, our Saviour.

In this chapter, we will consider 4 questions as they relate to the theme of "spiritual warfare"

Are there examples of this warfare in the Bible?
Can Christians be possessed by evil spirits?
What are our weapons to defeat this enemy?
What do these "powers of darkness" fear?
Will we witness their demise?

Let's begin by looking at spiritual warfare in the Bible. One of the most familiar and memorable examples of God's archangels involved in a battle with rebel spiritual beings is found in the book of Daniel 10:7-17. In this segment Daniel had been in deep intercessory prayer calling on God for help after having a revelation of an upcoming great war. After 3 weeks he was approached by an angel who explained why it had taken so long for him to come in response to his prayer. Here a bit of this conversation so you can see for yourself the heavenly war that was going on in verse 12-21,

> *"Then he continued, 'Do not be afraid, Daniel. Since the first day that you set your mind to gain understanding and to humble yourself before your God, your words were heard, and I have come in response to them. But the prince of the Persian kingdom resisted me 21 days. Then Michael, one of the chief princes (an Archangel) came to help me.'"* Daniel says, *"Again the one who looked like a man touched me and gave me strength...So he said 'Do you know why I have come to you? Soon I will return to fight against the prince of Persia (an enemy of God) and when I go, the prince of Greece (another enemy of God) will come; but first I will tell you what is written in the Book of Truth. (No one supports me against them except Michael your prince."*

In case you didn't catch it, this battle was going on between God's angels (including Michael) and spiritual powers of darkness (demons) exercising influence over the Persian realm and later on the Greek realm in the interests of Satan. Two kingdoms who came against Israel. This my friends is "spiritual warfare" in the heavenly realm.

Here is another example found in 2 Kings 6 where we see a servant of the prophet Elisha in great fear at seeing that an army with horses and chariots had surrounded their city. There were, however, an army of protectors that they couldn't see in the heavenly realm, ready to do battle for them in verses 16-17.

> *"'Don't be afraid,' the prophet answered. 'Those who are with us are more than those who are with them.' And Elisha prayed, 'O LORD, open his eyes so he may see.' Then the LORD opened the servant's eyes and he looked and saw the hills full of horses and chariots of fire all around Elisha (which is a description of the protecting might of the heavenly hosts).*

Yes, there are battles going on between the armies of God and the forces of evil in the heavenly realm. But what about here on earth? Are these powers of darkness at work and if so, our next question comes to mind: Can a Christian be demon possessed?

The New Testament makes it clear that a Christian cannot be owned or possessed by Satan or demons. That assurance comes from the fact that a born-again member of the Body of Christ is indwelt by the Holy Spirit and Christ. Romans 8:11 tells us,

> *"And if the Spirit of him who raised Jesus from the dead is living in you, he who raised Christ from the dead will also give life to your mortal bodies through his Spirit, who lives in you."*

Believers have been delivered from the domain of darkness and transferred to the kingdom of His beloved Son. Check this out in Colossians 1:13,

> *"For he has rescued us from the dominion of darkness and brought us into the kingdom of the Son he loves."*

That my friend is *good news!*

However, we also hear warnings of falling prey to these enemies. In 2 Timothy 2:26 Paul says,

> *"They will come to their senses and escape from the trap of the devil, who has taken them captive to do his will."* Ephesians 4:27 warns us, *"Do not give the devil a foothold."* In 1 John 3:8, the writer tells us, *"He who does what is sinful is of the devil."*

So, are we in a war? I would say yes we are. Listen to Peter's portrayal of Satan and what our defense should be:

> *"Be sober-minded, be watchful. Your adversary the devil prowls around like a roaring lion, seeking someone to devour. Resist him, firm in your faith, knowing that the same kinds of suffering are being experienced by your brotherhood throughout the world"* (1 Peter 5:8-9, ESV).

While Christians cannot be owned by Satan, an idea that derives from the unfortunate "possession" language, they can be attacked, which can take various forms: persecution, harassment, being captivated by false teaching and enslavement to sin.

You may have read about leaders and groups who take the idea of this warfare as a call to confront the spirit world. Be aware, we are never commanded to rebuke spirits and demand their flight in the name of Jesus. Their authority has already been withdrawn by the Most High in the crucifixion, resurrection and ascension of Jesus.

In Paul's explanation of spiritual warfare to the church at Ephesus in Chapter 6, nowhere does he recommend that believers confront or admonish the supernatural rulers, principalities, authorities or cosmic powers. His list of weapons does not include such things as exorcism against the spiritual forces of evil in the heavenly places. Instead, we are to **put on** the full Armor of God so we can take our stand against the enemy. In the verses noted, we find what Paul considered effective in this spiritual combat, what he refers to as armor:

- Truth – v. 14
- Righteousness – v. 14
- The Gospel – v. 15
- Faith – v. 16
- Salvation – v. 17
- The Word of God – v. 17
- Prayer – v. 18, 19, 20 (5 times in total)
- Perseverance – v.18

It is not difficult to see that instead of power encounters, spiritual warfare in this passage is about having persevering faith in the gospel and the Word of God and living a holy, prayerful life as a follower of Jesus. There are other passages that follow along with this teaching. One in particular I'd like to share with you found in 2 Corinthians 10:3-6, "*For though we live in the world, we do not wage war as the world does. The weapons we fight with are not the weapons of the world. On the contrary, they have divine power to demolish strongholds. We demolish arguments and every pretension that sets itself up against the knowledge of God, and we take captive every thought to make it obedient to Christ.*"

While not spectacular, adherence to truth and committed discipleship is what constitutes spiritual warfare in New Testament theology. Is that easy? Not so much. We need to prepare ourselves to avoid the attacks of the devil in the form of false teaching, temptation and sinful life patterns. Being obedient disciples is what makes us fit soldiers for Christ.

Now to the ultimate good news answer to the question "What do these powers of darkness fear and will we witness their demise?"

When the events of the final days begin to unfold, the devil will understand that his time is short. Revelation 12:12 says, "*Therefore rejoice, you heavens and you who dwell in them! But woe to the earth and the sea, because the devil has gone down to you! He is filled with fury, because he knows that his time is short."* He was powerless to resist being cast down, so he knows the Most High is superior. So why would the powers of darkness continue their evil work? The truth is, evil spirits are doing what is consistent with their character, plus they realize they have no opportunity of redemption so there is no point to change.

But the question was what do they fear? New Testament eschatology links the concept of "the fullness of the gentiles" to the return of Jesus. The second coming immediately precedes the day of the Lord and final judgment, which is the end for these powers of darkness. So just what is "the fullness of the gentiles?" The phrase refers to the evangelization of the world's nations. Matthew 24:14 (ESV) says, *"And this gospel of the kingdom will be proclaimed throughout the whole world as a testimony to all nations and then the end will come."*

The disinherited nations created at the judgment of Babel, which includes all nations today, must be reclaimed by the evangelism of their occupants. We also can see in Romans that the completion of Gentile evangelism is necessary for a softening and redemption of Paul's people, the Jews.

What this means for the question under consideration is that the ongoing evil activity of Satan, demons, and the fallen angels (gods) not yet imprisoned makes sense if the goal is impeding and forestalling the fullness of the gentiles. In other words, opposing world evangelism allows them more time to spread misery and destruction among humanity, the objects of God's love and plan, hence *their enemies.*

This is the only definable "victory" the powers of darkness can hope to accomplish. It is the only conceivable way they can hurt and grieve God. In this context, their resistance is understandable and Jesus' command, *"Go into all the world and proclaim the gospel to the whole creation"* (Mark 16:15, ESV). This is where we come in.

We are God's agents to bring about the "fullness of the gentiles" which will mean the end for these powers of darkness. No wonder they are so active in keeping people enslaved to false gods, idols, evil world powers, sinful lifestyles and away from the teachings of Jesus.

My friends, the battle rages, but the outcome is sure. Nothing is impossible with God; Satan and his followers are doomed. That is *good news!*

In the next chapter, we'll look at one of the tools discussed as part of the Armor of God—Prayer.

Question #12

WHAT IS PRAYER AND WHY CAN IT HELP US DEAL WITH THIS WORLD OF CHAOS?

We are still looking at Spiritual Warfare.

You'll remember I shared with you the teaching of Paul in the letter to the church of Ephesus that focused on The Armour of God and how we can combat the powers of darkness. Why is that important? Because they are the enemy of God and of mankind and are active in our world today. Can we doubt that as we see the mayhem happening all around us? It's also important to note the real damage is always done in the dark.

At the close of that chapter, we saw the call to prayer mentioned five times which tells me it's important, hence, the question we'll look at today, what is Prayer and why can it help us deal with this world of chaos?

To begin, I'd like to read the section I'm talking about from Ephesians 6:18-20. Watch for those five mentions of prayer:

> *"And pray in the Spirit on all occasions with all kinds of prayers and requests. With this in mind, be alert and always keep on praying for all the saints. Pray also for me, that whenever I open my mouth, words may be given me so that I will fearlessly make known the mystery of the gospel, for which I am an ambassador in chains. Pray that I may declare it fearlessly, as I should."*

Perhaps you already know what prayer is, but I would like to share with you a definition that I think puts it into perspective for us today. "Prayer in the Hebrew Bible is an evolving means of interacting with God, most frequently through a spontaneous, individual, unorganized form of petitioning and/or thanking…in these instances, such as with Isaac, Moses, Samuel and Job, the act of praying is a method of changing a situation for the better." See https://en.m.wikipedia.org

Two phrases in this definition bear looking at more closely.

First, "interacting with God." This is something God wants—His creation sharing their thoughts and needs with Him. Let's consider how He actually began this process way back in the Garden of Eden. Here were Adam and Eve right after having been led astray by the serpent to disobey God's command in Genesis 3:8-9, *"Then the man and his wife heard the sound of the LORD God as he was walking in the garden in the cool of the day, and they hid from the LORD God among the trees in the garden. But the LORD God called to the man, 'Where are you?'"* Hence the conversation began.

Even though Adam and Eve would be forever estranged from God and excommunicated from the Garden, they could still talk to God as those throughout the Bible did in a variety of ways. Many of God's priests, prophets, Kings and followers shared their deepest desires with God. They voiced their words of praise and worship to Yahweh—the one and only God. Like David, they cried out to God who was often asking for forgiveness for his sin as many others did throughout Scripture and there are many prayers that express words of gratitude and thanksgiving for all that God did for them in many situations of need.

Now to the second important phrase in the definition I shared, "changing a situation for the better."

Perhaps that is where we are today, in need of the God of the Universe to step in and change our situation for the better. But what might that look like?

I'd like to share with you two examples of God intervening in answer to prayer. Although there are a variety of stories I could share, even personal situations, I've chosen two from different centuries that I hope will encourage you.

Ever since the early believers felt the ground shake under them at prayer meeting in Acts 4:31 *"After they prayed, the place where they were meeting was shaken,"* Christians have realized that when they talk to God, things happen. The history of prayer certainly has had its ups and downs. No doubt, wars have been fought with both sides seeking divine assistance. Sometimes He grants exactly what's requested, however, often He has a better idea. Still Christian history is packed with earnest prayers and amazing answers.

This first example is entitled "Reviving New York," which may seem appropriate under the circumstances today.

One day in 1857 (which was not a good time for churches in downtown Manhattan) the North Dutch Reformed Church on Fulton Street resorted to creative measures, hiring a businessman named Jeremiah Lanphier as a sort of outreach minister. At first, he knocked on doors in the neighbourhood and distributed pamphlets and Bibles, but response generally was dismal. One day as he was walking along the streets, he wrote in his journal "the idea was suggested to my mind that an hour of prayer would be beneficial to businessmen." The idea blossomed: a weekly prayer time, open to anyone, bankers to broom-pushers was birthed. Come when you can, leave when you must. Handbills advertised the first meeting at noon on September 23rd, 1857.[10]

---

[10] http://movement.org/a-call-to-prayer-during-a-city-crisis/

Lanphier waited for the first attenders. No one showed up for the first 10 minutes, twenty, thirty. Then one man straggled in, then another. The hour ended with 6 men present, praying. The following week there were 20, the next week 40. Soon 100. Some of them wanted to meet every day. Rooms were packed. The church had to ask another church to handle the overflow. When churches ran out of room, the prayer meetings moved to theaters. By March 1858 (just 6 months later) the New York Times could report that Burton's Theater on Chambers Street was packed as a famous preacher Henry Ward Beecher led a crowd of 3,000 in prayer. Some estimated that up to a million people became Christians in the 1857-58 revival.

What caused such immense interest in prayer at this time? A stock market crash might have had something to do with it. Business leaders enslaved to money were suddenly seeking a more reliable master. When he started his humble prayer time, Jeremiah Lanphier had no way of knowing about the impending financial collapse. He just knew people needed to pray.

I might suggest such a time is fast approaching our world only it may actually be a global economic collapse. Could prayer be our answer?

Now I'd like to move forward to 1989, a century later and half a world away, another prayer meeting had an even greater effect on a society. For several years, four churches in Communist Leipzig, East Germany, had been holding weekly prayer meetings every Monday evening at 5 p.m. Political change was in the air during 1989 and these meetings began to grow.[11]

After the prayer meetings, people would light candles and walk peacefully through the city streets, a gentle protest against the communist regime. The peaceful protests grew. As many as 50,000 eventually joined in.

---

[11] www.dm.com/peace-prayers-helped-bring-down-the-wall-says-leipzig-pastor a-3805080

Then came October 9, what Germans began to call "the turning point." The East German government got involved, sending in police and soldiers with orders to shoot the protesters. Many feared a bloodbath. When one church opened its doors for the weekly prayer meeting, 2,000 Communist Party members rushed in to take all the seats. No problem: the church opened the balconies for the usual protesters and, like it or not, the Communists had to sit through a prayer meeting.

Did prayer silence the weapons? That's what many German Christians believe. Amazingly, shots weren't fired that night in Leipzig as 70,000 people marched peacefully through town. On the next Monday, when 120,000 marched, or the next, when there were 500,000 nearly the entire population of Leipzig!

In early November nearly a million marched through the capital, East Berlin. Police defied orders to shoot. The president resigned in disgrace. And soon there was an opening in the famous Berlin Wall. The stunning developments spread throughout Eastern Europe as peaceful resolutions dismantled Communist regimes. Whether or not prayers really move mountains, they certainly mobilized the population of Leipzig." Certainly, there were political and social undercurrents, but don't miss the spiritual dimension. It was obvious to the people most closely involved. A few weeks after that dramatic "turning point," someone put up a banner in Leipzig saying, "We thank you church."

As we listen to the mayhem in many cities in the United States that may continue to spread quickly in other cities as economic chaos and riots unfold, do we need prayer? Could prayer meetings leading to peaceful candle-lit quiet protests make a difference? Is this what God is looking for from his people?

I believe this is good news in our upside-down world. Only God can bring about a change of heart and minds. We need to intersect with God and call out for a change for the better.

As Paul shared in his letter to the church, we need to be alert and always keep on praying—on all occasions with all kinds of prayers and requests.

I take his request in verse 19 and 20 personally in my closing to this answer, as I've been doing regularly for some 14 months as this book has been written, *I ask God that whenever I open my mouth, words may be given me so that I will fearlessly make known the mystery of the gospel the Good News for which I am an ambassador in isolation. I pray that I may declare it as fearlessly as I should."*

Let us remember the wonderful promise in Matthew 18:20 spoken by Jesus, *"For where two or three gather in my name, there am I with them."*

That promise is what coming together in prayer means, Jesus will be in the midst. If we are to cope with this world of chaos, we need to know that God is calling out to us, to all of us. "Where are you?" He asks, just as He called out to Adam in the Garden of Eden. He wants us to share how much we love Him, our belief that He is listening, and that nothing is too difficult for Him.

So, my friends, may we call out like those believers way back in 1857 and 1989 to a God Who can move mountains to move in our world and bring an end to the chaos all around us.

"IF AND THEN" ANSWERS TO QUESTIONS OF THE DAY

Question #13

IS THERE A WAY TO OVERCOME WORRY AND ANXIETY?

As we unpack the verses that apply to this question, I often add 2 words—**If and Then.** Many years ago, I participated in a study that was entitled *My Part and God's Part* that helped me see the "if" as my part and the "then" as God's part.

So, let's get started! For each question we'll look at how it might relate to what we're going through in our own lives. Then we'll read the Scripture passage that provides an Answer to that Question.

I'll provide a brief overview of who wrote it and who it was written to and how it can help us today while emphasizing the "if" and "then."

This is our first question. "Is there a way to overcome worry and anxiety?" First, we need to understand why worry and anxiety (or stress) is on the increase in 2021. Listen to what the CDC says about it: [12]

Stress during an infectious disease outbreak can sometimes cause the following:

- Fear and worry about your own health and the health of your loved ones, your financial situation or job, or loss of support services you rely on.
- Changes in sleep or eating patterns.
- Difficulty sleeping or concentrating.

---

[12] www.cdc.gov/coronovirus/2019-ncov/daily-life-coping-managingstress-anxiety

- Worsening of chronic health problems and mental health conditions
- Increased use of tobacco and/or alcohol and other harmful substances.

If you are dealing with any of these symptoms, then I would say you need an answer to "how to cope" and "how to overcome."

Paul said to the Philippians:

> *"Do Not be anxious about anything, but in everything, by prayer and petition, with thanksgiving, present your requests to God. And the peace of God, which transcends all understanding, will guard your hearts and your minds in Christ Jesus." –Philippians 4:6-7*

Let's review this with the if and then added:

> *Do not be anxious about anything, but* ***if*** *in everything, by prayer and petition with thanksgiving, present your requests to God.* ***Then*** *the peace of God which transcends all understanding, will guard your hearts and your mind in Christ Jesus.*

Paul was most likely under house arrest when he wrote to the members of Philippi who were also experiencing a certain amount of persecution. That Paul understood how they were feeling—worried and anxious—was important in how he told them to overcome. It's like saying, "Been there, done that!"

You might consider this first piece of advice was pretty plain, *"Do not be anxious (or worry) about anything."* I guess I should just stop worrying, but between us, that's not so easy when things are like they are all around us and there seems to be no end to the reminders that we have little control over the future or how to fix the world's problems.

Paul realizes his readers need more so he shows us that *if* we need help, we need to do our part. *"In everything (not just in a few things but in everything) present your requests to God with Thanksgiving (an anecdote to worry)* then we hear the promise—God's Part, "*the peace of God* (an inner tranquility that only God can provide, the opposite of anxiety) "*that transcends all understanding" (*in other words that is beyond human understanding,) *"guards our hearts and our minds in Christ Jesus.*

I love this picture. It's a military picture, guards come and surround us and protect us from the enemy. He protects us from worry and anxiety. Do you like that picture?

In closing, yes, there is an answer to worry and anxiety, but remember, you have a part to play, and I can assure you God will do His part. There have been many times in my life when I was dealing with a variety of issues bringing me to a place of much worry and anxiety, but when I was reminded of this promise, I was blessed every time when I truly gave whatever I was dealing with to God in prayer.

Question #14

IS THERE SOMEONE I CAN TRUST WHEN I'M CONFUSED?

I'm assuming there are those reading this chapter who might be feeling confused, like me during these times of turmoil and uncertainty. I hear such conflicting advice from a variety of sources—which ones do I trust? No wonder we're confused. In the first chapter of this book, we looked at the question "Is there anybody in control?" Perhaps just another way of saying that is, "Is there someone I can trust?

Today we're going forward from that discussion to look at a verse that many of us may have heard and may have memorized. The issue is not hearing it, or even memorizing it, the issue is *living* it. This verse, written by Solomon (to whom God gave the gift of wisdom), is found in the Book of Proverbs Chapter 3 verses 5-6:

> *"Trust in the LORD with all your heart and lean not on your own understanding, in all your ways acknowledge Him and He will make your paths straight."*

Now I'd like to read it adding "if" and "then" which we talked about in the last chapter. Our Part and God's Part.

> *"**If** you trust in the Lord with all your heart and lean not on your own understanding and in all your ways acknowledge Him, **then** He will direct your paths."*

So let's see how this teaching, this "promise" can provide an answer to the question: "Is there someone I can trust when I'm confused?"

Take a few minutes to consider whether there is someone in your life who you totally trust, a spouse, a mother or father, or a friend. I can honestly say my mother was someone I trusted; I had total and complete confidence in her integrity, ability and good character because I knew her for 60 years. I knew she would always do what was best for me. Now I ask myself: is that the same level of trust I am placing in my Heavenly Father?

The first step in doing my part in this wisdom promise is to *"trust in Him with all my heart."* Imagine Job, a man who must have been confused about his situation. But here is his affirmation that he truly trusted God:

> *"Naked I came from my mother's womb, and naked I will depart. The LORD gave and the LORD has taken away; may the name of the LORD be praised"* (Job 1:21).

You see, this surrender leaves no room for confusion. Only God is perfectly trustworthy and faithful. So that is the first step in doing our part.

Step two is to *"lean not on our own understanding."* In other words, we must stop relying on ourselves, let go of what we think we know, and to let God take the wheel of what He perfectly knows. If you're a controlling person, that will not be easy. I actually believe that's why God lets confusing and troubling times come into our lives. We need to realize that we need Him and that we need to trust Him completely.

Step 1: Trust – Step 2: Lean

Step three is *"in all your ways acknowledge Him."* Note the word "all." It doesn't say "some" or "a few," it says "*all* our ways." This means we must admit we need Him everyday, in every way. Why? Because He cares. He's always available, He's always trustworthy, no matter the situation. I think about how it sometimes seems easy to believe God is Lord over our world but not always so easy to believe He's Lord over our heart.

But that, my friends, only happens when we let it. This is when He will begin to do His part.

Now to the Good News part, the Promise: *Then He will direct your paths.*

He will begin to establish our steps and lead us where He needs us, so we can move forward regardless of the circumstances. Is that always an easy path?

Imagine Joseph in the Bible when he had to face the fact that his brothers hated him enough to almost kill him. He then had to endure all that went with their foiled plot. We hear in his own words that he was actually trusting and believing that God was directing him where he needed to go. This is what he ultimately told those brothers:

> *"You intended to harm me, but God intended it for good to accomplish what is now being done, the saving of many lives" (Genesis 50:20).*

In the New Testament, we see that it wasn't easy for the Apostle Paul to be ridiculed, beaten, thrown in jail and ultimately killed because of his faith, but he knew that God had a plan and he marched forward, sharing the Gospel with all those He put in his path. Imagine sharing the Gospel with the guards who were put in charge of him while in prison. God was directing him where he needed him to go.

So, take a few minutes to consider if you're ready, to do your part, and then be ready to see God do His part, and be ready to stop being confused.

God created you. He loves you. He knows you better than you know yourself. The fact that He is all-knowing gives Him the ability to see what lies ahead and because of this, He knows what we need to fully be the ones He created us to be. Because of this, He also knows what needs to take place and which direction we need to go to receive the blessings He wants to give us.

Think about it. Ask God to remove the pride and stubborn independence from your heart. That has certainly been a major step for me and maybe for you too. Ask Him to place Proverbs 3:5-6 on your heart, soul and mind so you can live by it each and every day of your life.

> *"Trust in the LORD with all your heart, And lean not on your own understanding." –Proverbs 3:5-6*

Question #15

CAN I BE ASSURED SOMEONE WILL TAKE CARE OF MY NEEDS?

Before we investigate God's Word to find a good news answer to this question, let's consider what needs might concern us today.

As we reflect on the state of our world and the problems such as possible food shortages or lack of income due to lockdowns, what thoughts come into your mind? Perhaps you are wondering: *How am I going to support my family if I lose my job or my pension? What will happen if there is a shortage of food?* One prime example of food shortage is Venezuela.

I realize we aren't seeing this shortage yet in Canada and the U.S., but is it coming? We are hearing of many people who are struggling financially because of a lack of income and no savings to fall back on. If you are seeing and hearing about these things, I guess the question is, *"Can I be assured that there is someone who will take care of all my needs?"* Yes, there is. Let's look into Matthew 6:31-33 and see what Jesus has to say to us.

> *So do not worry, saying, "What shall we eat?" or "What shall we drink?" or "What shall we wear for clothing?" For the pagans run after all these things, and your heavenly Father knows that you need them. But seek first his kingdom and his righteousness, and all these things will be given to you as well."*

Let's consider once again the if and then in this verse. If you do not worry and you seek first his kingdom and his righteousness, then all these things will be given to you as well. *Again, our part and God's part.*

In the section leading up to this promise, Jesus makes a reference to how God looks after the birds of the air and the lilies of the field (what they will eat and what they will wear) and then reminds us, *"Are you not much more valuable than they?" (v. 26).*

In verse 31 we hear the first part of this promise, *"So do not worry."* If His advice stopped there you might say, *That's easy to say but not so easy to do. I'm not a bird or a lily, I'm a spouse, a mother or a father and I have a family who depend on me. I've tried to stop worrying but with all the warnings coming my way, it's not working.*

So, the second part in Verse 32 is important to remember: *"For the pagans run after all these things, and your heavenly Father knows that you need them."* Here is where Jesus reminds us how we are different than those who do not know God. We have Someone Who can not only supply all our needs, He knows what we need." I would suggest He even knows before we do. Here's an amazing example of this truth:

George Muller, who was known for providing for over 10,000 orphans in his lifetime, was advised by the housemother of one such orphanage he had built that there was no food for them to eat. He asked her to take the 300 children into the dining room and have them sit at the tables. Then he proceeded to thank God for the food and waited. He knew God would provide food for the children as He always did. Within minutes, a baker knocked on the door. "Mr. Muller," he said "I could not sleep. Somehow, I knew that you would need bread this morning. I got up and baked three batches for you. I will bring it in." This process continued with a milkman, whose cart had broken down in front of the orphanage and he didn't want to see the milk spoil so he knocked on their door and asked, "Would you like some milk?"[13]

---

[13] www.christianity.com/church/church-history/church-history-for-the-kids/george-mueller-orphanages-built-by-prayer-11634869

When Jesus said Your Heavenly Father "knows that you need them," this would be a prime example of that truth. God certainly knew far in advance that these 300 children would need food on that very day and made amazing arrangements to provide it far in advance.

Now to the "if" and "then" part of this verse. First off is our part, the ***if** we seek first his kingdom and his righteousness*. But what does that mean?

"Seek" here means to prioritize, to put God at the forefront of your thoughts, to seek the things of God as a *priority* over the things of the world. To do that my friends, we must know the mind of God. We need to open His Word daily and listen to His teaching about His Kingdom and His righteousness. I don't have the time in this chapter to go into all that those terms mean, but believe me, if you make the choice to put Him first and sincerely ask Him to show you the way—He will!

And now to God's part, ***then** all these things will be given to you.* Remember the promise here focuses on our *needs* not our *wants*. This was just what George Muller did on a daily basis. A practice that would have given him the assurance that God would provide for their needs.

It is no different in our world. Remember in the last chapter how we heard, *"in all your ways acknowledge Him"* that, my friends, is prioritizing. God is in control, and He wants us to know and be assured that He will take care of our needs.

So next time you're faced with wondering if there is someone who will take care of your needs, remember to put God first and let Him do the heavy lifting.

Question #16

HOW WILL WISDOM HELP US COPE WITH TRIALS?

As we consider the purpose of wisdom in helping us cope with trials, I'd like to begin by considering some advice given by James, a brother of Jesus and the "shepherd" of the early believers in Jerusalem.

He knew that it's relatively easy to live as a Christian when things are calm, and all is well. But it's a much more difficult prospect when the storms of life hit with full force. At such times, it's easy to get off course or even to lose our faith.

His readers were facing various difficult trials. They were dispersed abroad mostly due to persecution. They had suffered the loss of their homes and possessions. Many were not able to escape persecution even in the places to which they fled. James wanted them to know how to navigate through these trials and this testing of their faith so that they would be able to persevere, resulting in maturity. But even more that they would consider it pure joy, in other words he wanted them to *joyfully* endure.

There is a basic ingredient we all need to endure trials joyfully. That may not be your goal during these times of trials and challenges\ but let me assure you it is God's goal. Otherwise, He wouldn't be allowing them to come into our lives. We need God's wisdom; thus, He gives us this teaching:

> *"If any of you lacks wisdom, he should ask God, who gives generously to all without finding fault and it will be given to him. But when he asks, he must believe and not doubt,*

because he who doubts is like a wave of the sea, blown and tossed by the wind."–James 1:5-6

Wisdom here refers to what we need to endure trials with God's joy, which usually goes against our natural inclination. When trials hit, we're all prone to ask *why*. The important question we should be asking is how. *"How can I understand this trial from God's perspective? How can this trial help me grow in maturity?"*

Pastor Warren Wiersbe talks about his secretary who was going through difficult trials. She had a stroke, her husband had gone blind, and then he had to be taken to the hospital where, as far as they knew, he would die. When Pastor Wiersbe was assuring her that he was praying that God would help and strengthen her he was startled when she said, "I appreciate that, but pray about one more thing, that I'll have the wisdom not to waste all of this!"[14]

Let's consider that for ourselves today, our need for wisdom and what James and Pastor Warren are telling us:

Is there an if (our part)? Yes there is! We are to *"ask God…and believe and not doubt."*

Step 1—Ask God. To do this we must humble ourselves and admit that we don't know what we need to live joyfully in the face of trial.

Step 2—Ask in faith (believing without doubt). God doesn't give wisdom to everyone in the world, but rather to every believer in Christ who asks in faith. It's impossible to please God, for he who comes to God must believe that He exists, that He personally cares, and He is able to give the wisdom that he needs to endure trials with joy.

---

[14] www.vvdailypress.com/news/20200215 (references Warren Wiersbe and his conversation with his secretary in his Bible Commentary)

Now the question: Is there a then (God's part)? Absolutely there is, "*He gives generously without finding fault.*" Why? Because He loves us and loves to provide for our needs!

To illustrate God's part, I'd like to share a wonderful example of that truth written by Joni Erickson Tada who at the age of 17 was paralyzed from the neck down in a diving accident, she said:

> *"God engineered the circumstances. He used them to prove Himself—as well as my loyalty. Not everyone has this privilege. I felt there were only a few people God cared for in such a special way that He would trust them with this kind of experience. This understanding left me relaxed and comfortable as I relied on His love, exercising newly learned trust. I saw that my injury was not a tragedy but a gift God was using to help me conform to the image of Christ, something that would mean my ultimate satisfaction, happiness – even joy."*[15]

That, my friends, is a clear example of how God's wisdom can help someone endure a major trial with joy! She didn't get that wisdom from the world. She didn't make it up herself. It came from God, through His Word. If you need God's wisdom for how to endure any major or minor trial with joy, ask Him in faith and He will give it.

---

[15] Joni (Zondervan) page 154

Question #17

HOW DO WE KNOW GOD LOVES US?

This morning as I was working on this chapter, I asked my husband that question and his answer was simply "Because the Bible tells me so." He always has such a clear understanding of truth and I hope as we look into God's Word, we'll see what he meant.

When life becomes overwhelming, when you sit alone, head in your hands, you may think to yourself, *where is God now?* When tears are spilling down your cheeks, when you just lost your job, or a close friend, or your house because you don't have enough money to pay the mortgage, or maybe you've just lost hope in what's ahead for you, this question is normal.

Maybe you're fed up with who you are, you think you are not worthy of His love. There are unlimited reasons that can cause a person to doubt God's love, to question if He even cares.

That's why I chose to look at this question today. When these kinds of thoughts loom and threaten to overwhelm you, the best possible prescription is to turn to the one place that is reliable and trustworthy, the Word of God. The second chapter in this book provided clear teaching as to why we can depend on it. If need be go back and be reminded.

There is abundant proof that God loves you! Let's begin by looking into some of David's words found in the Psalms where we will hear a few wonderful truths about God's Love.

> *"But, you O Lord are a compassionate and gracious God, slow to anger abounding in love and faithfulness."–Psalm 86:15*

"He does not treat us as our sins deserve or repay us according to our iniquities. For as high as the heavens are above the earth, so great is his love for those who revere him." –Psalm 103:10-11

"Your love, O Lord, reaches to the heavens…How priceless is your unfailing love, O God!"–Psalm 36:5,7

Going on a little further in the Old Testament we see the Prophet Jeremiah sharing words from God Himself in Jeremiah 31:3,

"The Lord appeared to us in the past, saying, "I have loved you with an everlasting love; I have drawn you with loving-kindness."

What we've heard so far about God's love is that He is abounding in love, a great, unfailing and everlasting love.

We are also privileged to hear all about God's love in the New Testament letter written by John the Apostle and it's so clear and so concise.

"Dear Friends, let us love one another, for love comes from God. Everyone who loves has been born of God and knows God. Whoever does not love does not know God, because God is love. This is how God showed his love among us: He sent his one and only Son into the world that we might live through him. This is love, not that we loved God, but that he loved us and sent his son as an atoning sacrifice for our sins." –1 John 4:7-10

Another verse that tells just how much He loves us is found in *Romans 5:8,*

"But God demonstrates his own love for us in this: While we were still sinners Christ died for us."

A quick summary:

1. Love comes from God
2. God is Love
3. He loves us so much that while we were still sinners, He sent his son to die on a cross for us and that by believing and trusting in Him we can be saved and assured of eternal life with Him.
4. A surprise truth here is that we can't do anything to *earn* God's love, it's all about believing and trusting.

An affirmation to help us when we are dealing with so many trying times is found in Romans 8:35,37 that assures us that we're safe. Listen to Paul's teaching: *"Who shall separate us from the love of Christ? Shall trouble or hardship or persecution or famine or nakedness or danger or sword? No in all these things, we are more than conquerors through him who loved us."*

In closing consider this, He loves us so much that *He makes himself available to us whenever we reach out to him in prayer.* We know this because He has promised to hear them. Even if He doesn't always answer the way we think He should, He still hears us.

The Psalmist declared in Psalm 55:16-17, *"As for me, I call to God…and he hears my voice."*

My friends, don't be discouraged, instead thank God for His love for you and learn to commit everything to Him in prayer and believe that whatever the answer, it's the best answer because He loves you and He knows what's best.

Remember this beautiful verse from Romans 5:5, *"And hope does not put us to shame, because God's love has been poured into our hearts through the Holy Spirit, who has been given to us."* God never wants us to forget He loves us and once we come into that saving relationship with Jesus, His Holy Spirit reminds us of this. How grateful I am to know this, *Blessed Assurance, Jesus is Mine!*

A song many of us learned in Sunday School, "Jesus loves me, this I know, for the Bible tells me so" is also a reminder of God's love. Let's make sure our children are still hearing that little song because you never know just when they might need that wonderful assurance in the days ahead.

I hope these wonderful words from God have been encouraging for you today. Never doubt this message is from God!

GOD LOVES YOU

Question #18

WHY SHOULD I BE THANKFUL DURING THIS TRIAL?

A special day for Canadians in October is Thanksgiving. I've chosen this question because I'm aware it may be hard for many of us to be thankful in this upside-down world, yet the Apostle Paul gives the directive in 1 Thessalonians 5:16-18 to

> *"be joyful always, pray continually; give thanks in all circumstances, for this is God's will for you in Christ Jesus."*

Paul knew that people are naturally happy on some occasions, however, the Christian's joy is not dependent on circumstances.

Let's review some questions and answers we've already covered for a few reasons to be thankful.

Is There anyone in Control? Yes! The Creator who has existed from the beginning of time and space. He not only created everything but is far wiser than any human; He is in control. We can be thankful for this because our world is in trouble, and we need the reassurance there is someone who has a plan and is able to carry it out.

Where can I get reliable answers about the One in control? The Bible is the source of all we need to know about God the Creator—the One in control. We can be thankful for this because He provided it and He has given us all we need to both understand and accept whatever comes our way.

Is there good news in times of Personal Chaos? I shared the reason I've been thankful every day for the past 30 years. There is no more amazing answer to the trials of today than what I experienced following a terrible time of chaos. Good news is available to everyone!

If God is in control, why is there so much evil in our world? There were three rebellions by the original rebel, Satan, and the other adversaries in the Spiritual Realm. Spiritual warfare between the One True God (Yahweh) and these rebels is what's causing the evil. We can be thankful that God provided a solution.

But then we looked at God's solution to these problems—Jesus—His birth, death and resurrection.

Where Do religions come from and why should we trust Christianity over them?

We looked into many other religions and found there are real supernatural beings behind them who we must recognize as contenders against the true God—Yahweh. Christians believe in the one, eternal God. They believe He came to earth in human form, provided a way for people to be forgiven of their sin, and said that anyone who believed in Him would have eternal life. That is truly a wonderful reason to be thankful. You see I know that I'm a sinner in need of God's forgiveness and like everyone ever born, I will one day die and am so grateful I have the blessed assurance of eternal life in Heaven.

How do I find Internal peace in this world of chaos?

We looked at the lives of Joni Eareckson Tada, Fanny Crosby and Horatio Gates. When we face trials and tribulations, having wonderful examples like them is something to be thankful for.

There are other questions you might like to review that we have studied – all that will bring you to a place of being thankful, a place of gratitude. I think of one in particular – How do we know that God Loves us?

I'm grateful today for my husband, family, friends, church family, neighbours, but most of all for my Lord and Saviour Jesus Christ. In the month of April, I celebrated my 31st born-again birthday. To have been blessed to be able to share God's truth with others as a pastor and mentor. I'm especially grateful this year that God opened the door for me to write this book and to share with others even when we've been locked away from the world.

May God touch your lives with such love and power that you will never have to ask the question again.

QUESTIONS ON GOD'S PROMISES

Question #19

IS THERE ANYONE WHOSE PROMISES I CAN BELIEVE?

As of late, I've actually become very disillusioned with our society, especially as it relates to trust. There used to be places we could go to hear truth and to be able to believe promises. However, it seems those places or people are no longer trustworthy and promises made *will* be broken or are blatant lies. I'm referring to political leaders, the media, online bloggers, authors, some gurus and celebrities with hidden agendas, and even some preachers and teachers.

If I am feeling disillusioned, maybe you are as well. I've heard many friends in the last few months say they have tuned out the news (fake and otherwise). They say it's just too depressing and it seems you just can't believe anybody anymore. Some have even stopped watching sporting events because of political agendas there as well.

So, is there anyone whose promises we can believe? Yes, there is! In Chapter 2, we looked at where we could go to get reliable and trustworthy answers about God, and the answer was the Bible, confirmed by Archeological and Scientific evidence.

I will be referring to a number of Bible Verses that refer to God's promises and their reliability which is where I want to begin this series.

In future chapters, I will be delving into actual promises and how you can be uplifted and reassured so you can cope with all the dishonesty and agendas we are bombarded with every day.

So, let's begin by going to some passages in the Old Testament that remind us God fulfills His promises, He completes His work, and He will not abandon His plans for us:

> *"God is not human, that he should lie, not a human being that he should change his mind; Does he speak and then not act or does he promise and not fulfill?" –Numbers 23:19*

> *"Blessed be the LORD who has given rest to his people Israel, according to all that he has promised. Not one word has failed of all his good promises, which he spoke by Moses his servant. –1 Kings 8:56, ESV*

> *"Not one of all the Lord's good promises to Israel failed, everyone was fulfilled. –Joshua 21:45*

> *"Now I am about to go the way of all the earth. You know with all your heart and soul that not one of all the good promises the Lord your God gave you has failed. Every promise has been fulfilled; not one has failed. –Joshua 23:14*

> *"The Lord said to me, "You have seen correctly, for I am watching to see that my word is fulfilled. –Jeremiah 1:12*

> *"The Lord has done what he planned; he has fulfilled his word, which he decreed long ago" –Lamentations 2:17a*

> *"I will not violate my covenant or alter the word that went forth from my lips." –Psalm 89:34, ESV*

> *"Therefore say to them, 'This is what the Sovereign LORD says: None of my words will be delayed any longer; whatever I say will be fulfilled, declares the Sovereign LORD." –Ezekiel 12:28*

Just a few wonderful affirmations that God's Promises have all been fulfilled from the lips of Old Testament Patriarchs and Prophets.

NOW TO THE NEW TESTAMENT

> *"He who calls you is faithful; he will surely do it." –1 Thessalonians 5:24, ESV*

> *"The Lord is not slow to fulfill his promise as some count slowness, but is patient toward you, not wishing that any should perish, but that all should reach repentance." –2 Peter 3:9, ESV*

> *"Yet he (Abraham) did not waver through unbelief regarding the promise of God but was strengthened in his faith and gave glory to God, being fully persuaded that God had power to do what he had promised." –Romans 4:20-21*

> *"I am the Lord's servant,' Mary answered, 'May your word (or God's Promise) to me be fulfilled.' Then the angel left her.'" –Luke 1:38*

> *"Being confident of this, that he who began a good work in you will carry it on to completion until the day of Christ Jesus." –Philippians 1:6*

> *"For no matter how many promises God has made they are 'yes' in Christ." –2 Corinthains 1:20a*

> *"a faith and knowledge resting on the hope of eternal life, which God, who does not lie, promised before the beginning of time." –Titus 1:2*

This last reference seems very appropriate for our day, see if you agree:

> *"His divine power has given us everything we need for a godly life through our knowledge of him who called us by his own glory and goodness. Through these he has given us his very great and precious promises, so that through them you may participate in the divine nature, having escaped the corruption in the world caused by evil desires."*
> *–2 Peter 1:3-4*

In closing, I recommend you turn to Psalm 119, a wonderful Psalm that has 176 verses proclaiming the inerrancy and importance of reading, studying, and living by the Word of God. Let's look at a few of them. In verses 41-42, God says,

> *"May your unfailing love come to me, O Lord, your salvation according to your promise, then I will answer the one who taunts me, for I trust in your word."* And check out verse 140, *"Your promises have been thoroughly tested, and your servant loves them."* And finally in verse 148, *"My eyes stay open through the watches of the night that I may meditate on your promises."*

I hope that as you lay down your head tonight that you will turn to God's Word, even if it's just to read Psalm 119 in its entirety, meditating on the promises of God that are forever *true.*

In the next chapters, we'll be looking at verses that are actual promises. Some of these verses involve two words we might often overlook but that will lead us to remember God has a plan and He wants us to know it and live by the promises and warnings found in the Bible. Those two words I focused on previous chapters—*if* and *then.*

Question #20

HOW CAN GOD KEEP ALL HIS PROMISES?

In the last chapter, I addressed the question "Is there anyone whose promises I can believe?" by referring to several verses in the Bible that affirm the answer—yes, there is! Let's continue by looking at what can be considered the 10 types of promises in the Bible that we will look at over the next few chapters.

1. Promises about God's power.
2. Promises that God answers prayers.
3. Promises for God's guidance.
4. Promises for strength to do God's will.
5. Promises for forgiveness.
6. Promises for the Holy Spirit.
7. Promises for a changed heart.
8. Promises for victory over sin.
9. Promises for healing.
10. Promises for being God's witnesses.

Imagine—there is Someone Who not only can but *will* keep all His promises. Someone you can depend on no matter what.

Let's begin by looking at the first of those 10 types of promises that answers the question, "How can God keep all His promises?" I've chosen to look at the promise about God's power first because if we're going to believe things like "God will protect me," "He will be my strength," and "He will provide for me," then I would suggest we believe He has the *power* to accomplish them.

We will start at the beginning in Genesis 1:1 where we read about our all-powerful God right out of the gate! God wanted us to see who He is and how He can fulfill what He promises us throughout the rest of His Word.

> *"In the beginning God created the heavens and the earth. Now the earth was formless and empty, darkness was over the surface of the deep and the Spirit of God was hovering over the waters."*

There was only one person involved in the creation of our universe, and that was God. From that opening onward we see these words, repeatedly *"And God said."* That is power—being able to speak a world into existence—which by the way includes every living creature and mankind.

The idea of our existence arising from a primordial soup, alien beings, technological experiment or whatever conjecture we might hear on the television or internet is a long way from *"And God said…"* Why would we not want to believe in a creator God?

Let's continue to Genesis 18. Here we see God talking to Abraham after Sarah laughs at the promise that she and Abraham would have a child. They were both way beyond child-bearing age and didn't believe it was possible. So, God shared this promise with him in verse 14, *"Is anything too hard for the LORD? I will return to you at the appointed time next year and Sarah will have a son."* The key part of this verse for us today is this same question God asked Abraham, *"Is anything too hard for the LORD?"* That, my friends, is key to believing God can do anything. Later in Mark 10:27, we see Jesus reassuring His disciples when they question Him, *"Who then can be saved?"* This question comes after Jesus tells them that *"It is easier for a camel to go through the eye of a needle than for a rich man to enter the kingdom of God."* Here is His answer *"With man this is impossible, but not with God – all things are possible with God."*

Note the claim here, *all_things* are possible with God. This is a definite affirmation of God's Power.

There are other places in God's Word where people confirm His power. Let's go back into the book of Job. If you don't know Job's situation, take some time to consider the awful trials and tribulations he went through. He lost his family, his home and all his possessions, his health, and his reputation, but here in the last chapter of the book, we see him responding to God who has spent chapters 38—41 telling Job exactly who He is and what He's done. In other words, Job is getting a history lesson on God's Power. Take a few minutes and read through this section. Sometimes we need a history lesson.

In response, Job replies *"I know that you can do all things, no plan of yours can be thwarted."* (Job 42: 1-2). Wow! This is his response *before* verses 10-16, *"The Lord blessed the latter part of Job's life more than the first" (verse 12).* Job heard God and believed Him even *before* his life turned back around.

Now we turn to Romans 8: 31-32 and read Paul's teaching,

> *"If God is for us, who can be against us? He who did not spare his own Son, but gave him up for us all—how will he not also, along with him, graciously give us all things?"*

You see, no matter what trouble you might be in, no matter how many enemies you have chasing you, no matter if it's the devil himself giving you grief, remember these words *"If God is for us who can be against us?"*

In Jeremiah 10:12, we are told,

> *"But God made the earth by his power, he founded the world by his wisdom and stretched out the heavens by his understanding."*

This was Jeremiah the prophet telling those of Israel who were following false gods who the true God really was!

Listen to this verse

> *"By his power God raised the Lord from the dead, and he will raise us also."* (1 Corinthians 6:14).

That is power! I sure don't know of anybody other than God who can raise someone from the dead.

The last passage I'd like to share with you relating specifically to God's power to keep His promises comes from Isaiah 40:10, 28 who is encouraging God's people who have gone through great distress.

> *"See the Sovereign Lord comes with power and he rules with a mighty arm...Do you not know? Have you not heard? The Lord is the everlasting God, the Creator of the ends of the earth. He will not grow tired or weary and his understanding no one can fathom."*

My friends, there are so many verses providing us with the assurance that God is powerful that I would never have time to share them all with you in this short book, but if you'd like to do some of your own research, I suggest you find a biblical concordance, look for the word "power" and be prepared to be blessed, amazed and encouraged.

In the next chapter, we'll move along to the question: How do we know that God Answers Prayer? In this segment we will see a multitude of examples of this promise, and I will share with a couple of my own experiences.

Question #21

HOW DO WE KNOW THAT GOD ANSWERS PRAYER?

I'm hoping you have been encouraged so far in this series to hear that *yes* there is Someone Whose promises we can believe and then to hear that He has the power to keep those promises.

Today we move on to another of the 10 types of promises in the Bible, answering the Question: How do we know that God answers prayer?

This is a good news answer, my friends. When we ask Him to be with us, to protect us, to be our strength, to provide for us, to give us peace, to love us and to assure us that we will live with Him forever in Heaven, we need to be assured that God not only hears our prayers, but that He answers them.

So, let's move along for confirmation of this promise by realizing there are 3 ways God answers.

Yes, no, and not now.

God answers yes to many prayers. Sometimes yes comes in the form of confirmation. For example, if you ask the Lord a question and as you are reading in your Bible a "random" scripture addresses your prayer or concern in a very real and concrete way. You also might be amazed when you're handed an answer through talking with a friend and he or she brings up the subject out of the blue, and presto they share a word from the Lord and it's just what you needed to hear.

I feel it's important to note that God never answers yes to any request that goes against His Word or His will. If in our quest for an answer that seems to be what we want and not what God would want for us, and we think we hear yes, be assured, that answer is *not* from God.

Now the hard answer from God is no. This is not what we want to hear. We want God's blessing for our desires. But many times, no is the answer that comes. What often happens in this circumstance is that later, we actually see that no was the right answer. The prayer request was not what would have been good for us and if we're honest, we see that His no was a blessing. God's answer is *always* best.

And to the last answer, not now. This is probably the most frustrating and disappointing; it is also the one that requires the most patience. And that is not always what we think we need.

In the Spring of 1993, when my husband and I were expecting to receive word of our first church appointment, we expected it would begin in July of that year. Of course, we prayed fervently every day for the call. Imagine our disappointment when the answer was "not now." We had to wait until January 1994 when we unexpectedly got our answer and my friends, it was the best answer there could have been. We packed up and moved to Winnipeg where we were blessed to pastor a wonderful group of people for 7 ½ years. It was the perfect place for us. God answered our prayers in the very best way. That "not now" has sustained us over the years in some other situations where a yes was hoped for, but a not now was best.

It has taught me not to treat God like a genie in a bottle. I have learned to accept no and not now as a part of His plan for my life. Proverbs 3:5-6 tells us to

> *"trust in the LORD with all (our) heart and lean not on our own understanding, in all (our) ways submit to him and he will direct (our) paths."*

Regardless of the answer, His plan is always best. He has never steered me wrong and that's why I'm so happy to share a number of verses that not only confirm God *does* answer prayer, but have become promises I have claimed many, many times over the years.

> *"Do not be anxious about anything, but in everything, by prayer and petition, with thanksgiving, present your requests to God. And the peace of God, which transcends all understanding, will guard your hearts and your minds in Christ Jesus." –Philippians 4:6-7*

This promise confirms that God wants us to present our requests to Him especially those things that we're worried about—meaning He hears them—and that regardless of the actual outcome, He promises to give us peace about the situation. What an amazing picture! Every time I've claimed this promise, I picture in my mind God placing a guard around my heart and my mind giving me a peace about the situation even if God's answer to my specific request is no or not now.

There is a verse in Psalms I use at least once a week as I sit before the Lord in the request section of my prayer journal.

> *"Delight yourself in the Lord, and he will give you the desires of your heart." –Psalm 37:4*

Many years ago I heard a pastor preach on this verse and it has helped me ever since to understand that the promise *"and he will give you the desires of your heart"* is not a blanket yes to whatever I *think* I need but it's God's way of saying He will place desires in my heart that are His desires and when we come to Him in prayer asking for those things, the answer will be a resounding yes!

Here is a word from God to Jeremiah the Prophet while he was being confined,

> *"Call to me and I will answer you, and will tell you great and hidden things that you have not known." –Jeremiah 33:3, ESV*

Another verse that I also claimed for myself some 30 years ago and many times since is 1 John 1:9 (ESV),

> *"If we confess our sins, he is faithful and just to forgive us our sins and to cleanse us from all unrighteousness."*

This is not a no or a not now, this is a resounding yes! He hears and answers prayer.

Psalm 145:18 encourages us that God answers prayer, *"The Lord is near to all who call on him, to all who call on him in truth."*

Listen to this testimony of the Psalmist in Psalm 66:16-19,

> *"Come and listen, all you who fear God; let me tell you what he has done for my soul. I cried out to him with my mouth; his praise was on my tongue. If I had cherished sin in my heart, the Lord would not have listened, but God has surely listened and heard my voice in prayer."*

It's vital to note the progression here: First he "delighted in the Lord (his praise was on my tongue) and second, he realized he had to be free from sin and lastly, he could be assured that God listened and heard his prayer.

Again, there are so many passages and testimonies in the Bible confirming that yes, God always answers prayer, but I hope these few that we've looked at are an encouragement and helpful in those times you come before the Lord with your petitions.

Sometime in 2002, I was led to read a book by Becky Terrabassi, *Let Prayer Change Your Life,* that to this day reminds me of the amazing truth that God answers prayer as I use a journal she developed. [16] I begin each day as follows:

---

[16] Becky Terrabassi, *Let Prayer Change Your Life Publisdher Thmas Nelson Publishers November 19, 1999*

- Praising God for who He is.
- Confessing any sin that would hinder approaching His throne of grace.
- Requesting what I believe to be what is in His will.
- Thanking Him for answered prayer—whether that answer is yes, no or not now.

Before we move along to the next chapter where I'll be sharing with you the promise of God's guidance, let's be reminded of what we've learned so far in this series: There is Someone Whose promises we can believe Who has the power to keep all His Promises and that yes, He *does* answer prayer.

Question #22

WILL GOD PROVIDE US WITH GUIDANCE?

There is definitely a good news answer to this question. Imagine the One Who knows what's best for us will provide us with the guidance we need to get to that place.

If I were to look back at my life, I recognize God's guidance in so many ways. Even during the times I was wandering far away from Him. The first example would be when I was drowning in fear and anxiety not knowing which way to turn. My marriage was in jeopardy and a business I had started was failing miserably. But the good news is that God spoke into my heart and led me to my first true church home, The Salvation Army in Mississauga. I knew from the very first time I entered their door that I was in the right place to find my way out of distress, even though at the time I didn't know Jesus as my Lord. God led me to Himself and from that day forward, He has led my husband and I repeatedly. He has guided us in the way we should go, and I am to this day, 30 years down the road, blessed to be able to share some of these verses that promise guidance, reminding you that there is Someone Who not only keeps all His promises, but He guides us along a path only He knows is best for us.

We'll begin this journey into His promises to guide us back at the call of Abram in Genesis 12:1-2,

> *"The Lord had said to Abram, 'Leave your country, your people and your father's household and go to the land I will show you."*

That, my friends, is an example of God's promise of guidance and later in verse 4, we hear Abram's response,

> *"So Abram left, as the Lord had told him."*

God didn't tell him *where* he was leading him, just that he was to *go*, and Abram, who was 75 years of age at the time, trusted in God to show him—to guide him.

Later in Isaiah 30:21, we hear the Prophet sharing a promise for the people of Israel who had been living in opposition to God's teaching.

> *"Whether you turn to the right or to the left, your ears will hear a voice behind you saying, 'This is the way, walk in it.'"*

That was a promise we also need to heed. How many times does the Holy Spirit speak into our hearts, "This is the way, walk in it." Do we listen and follow? That is one of the ways God guides us, even today.

Let's turn now to the Psalms 32:8,

> *"I will instruct and teach you in the way you should go. I will counsel you and watch over you."*

Wow, a promise that God will instruct, teach, counsel, *and* watch over us! I would say that's a pretty good description of guidance, wouldn't you? However, the passage leading up to this promise is a call to turn from sin and find forgiveness and all that goes with it. A testimony psalm by David who knew all about the perils of not following God's guidance but wanted us to know of the blessings of being led by God to the place of forgiveness.

Another wonderful passage in the Psalms is found in one you most likely will be familiar with Psalm 23. I have this Psalm written out in my prayer journal with the following notations that bless me every time I read them. You may find this practice a blessing to you as well:

> *The Lord is my* shepherd (current and personal), *He makes me to lie down in green pastures (He's in control), he leads me beside quiet waters (like a shepherd, he leads, he doesn't drive me), he restores my soul when I am in need, He guides me in paths of righteousness" (it's still my choice).*

Another passage you may be familiar with is found in the book of Proverbs, *"Trust in the Lord with all your heart and lean not on your own understanding. In all your ways acknowledge Him and He will direct your paths"* (Proverbs 3:5-6). Hear the promise, He will direct your paths, in other words guide you. But don't forget the *if* in this passage *"(If you) trust in the Lord with all your heart and lean not on your own understanding."*

I'd like to close with two New Testament passages focusing on God's promise of guidance. Probably one of my favourites is found in Romans 8:28,

> *"And we know that in all things God works for the good of those who love him, who have been called according to His purpose."*

God calls us and guides us according to His purpose. A promise I've seen fulfilled throughout my journey over these 30 years as I've trusted in Him and loved Him.

And in closing, listen to John the Apostle in Revelation 7:17 as he sees believers gathered in Heaven before God's throne of grace,

> *"For the lamb at the center of the throne will be their shepherd; he will lead them to springs of living water. And God will wipe away every tear from their eyes."*

Imagine, we will be in heaven, led by Jesus, the good Shepherd to a place of eternal peace and security. No more tears and no more fears. I pray every day that those who are drowning in distress will come to know the Lord and trust in His promises.

I hope you are encouraged once again to reflect upon one of God's amazing Promises—His promise of guidance. One more definite promise we can believe was given to us by the only One Who can keep it. I hope you're looking forward to looking into His promise to provide us with the strength to do His will.

Question #23

WILL GOD PROVIDE US WITH THE STRENGTH WE NEED?

I hope you were encouraged to discover that God guides us, He directs our paths, He instructs and teaches us in the way we should go, and He will counsel and watch over us.

Now we move along to the promise for the strength to do God's will, to follow that path.

Remember that this promise is focused on our doing God's will, not our sometimes selfish will.

We hear this reminder in the letter written by Paul to the church of Philippi.

> *"For it is God who works in you (strengthens us) both to will and to act according to His good pleasure." –Philippians 2:13, NKJV*

In Philippians 4:13, we read

> *"I can do all things through Christ who strengthens me."*

I think this is another one of my favorite Scripture verses. I know it's not me who answered my prayers for guidance or for strength when I was being challenged beyond my abilities, it was Christ who provided me with the strength, to do His will even when I felt weak and helpless.

You may notice I used the term "weak" and once again, we find Gods promise of strength coming into play, spoken by Jesus Himself,

> *"But He said to me, 'My grace is sufficient for you, for my power is made perfect in weakness.'"* What was Paul's response? The same as my own only put much more eloquently *"Therefore I will boast all the more gladly about my weaknesses, so that the power of Christ may rest upon me"* (2 Corinthians 12:9, ESV).

We are not called to pretend we are strong, to brag about our abilities no matter how difficult the problem we may be facing, or to think that our educational degrees, our family heritage, our speaking or teaching skills, or our personalities are all that we need. No, the truth is we need to be like Paul. We are called to boast about our weaknesses, giving Christ the glory Whose power rests upon us; when we are weak, He is strong.

In Psalm 27:14 (NKJV), we read another part of this promise,

> *"Wait on the Lord, be of good courage and He shall strengthen your heart, wait I say on the LORD."*

Again, this is a strong recommendation. We know it's important because it's repeated, "Wait on the Lord."

Are you good at waiting? I'm not. I would prefer to come to God for the strength I need and *presto* there it is. But that's not what this passage tells us, it says wait. So, as well as recognizing our weakness, we are to wait. The Promise is God will provide us with the strength we need in His time, and we must remember this as well, we must do His will.

To close this chapter, I'd like to share a short passage from Isaiah that I believe is very encouraging for everyone needing God's strength.

> *"He gives strength to the weary and increases the power of the weak. Even youths grow tired and weary and young*

men stumble and fall; but those who hope in the LORD (meaning those who trust and are expectant) will renew their strength. They will soar on wings like eagles, they will run and not grow weary, they will walk and not be faint."–Isaiah 40:29-31

The word renew means to exchange like a change of clothing. In other words, their weakness will give way to God's strength.

Use that picture if it helps you to remember God's promise to provide you with the strength you need to do His will. You can take off that clothing representing weakness and God will provide you with His strength.

If you'd like to hear more about God's promise for strength, go to your Bible's concordance and look up some other wonderful passages that focus on the term "strength" and enjoy.

In the next chapter, we'll move along to the promise of forgiveness, and just in case you might think that promise is not for you, be sure my friends, the Bible tells us

"we have all sinned and fall short of the glory of God" (Romans 3:23).

Question #24

DOES GOD PROMISE TO FORGIVE US?

All the promises of God are true. Let's review:

- God promises to do what He says He'll do
- God answers prayers
- God will provide us guidance
- God will provide strength to do His will

Let's look at God's promise of forgiveness and how we all need to be forgiven. Now you might say, maybe you, do but I'm okay. I've never killed anybody, I'm pretty honest (most of the time), I don't steal and when I look around at my community, I'm better than most people I know so why do I need forgiveness?

Here is what God says in 1 John 1:8,

> *"If we claim to be without sin, we deceive ourselves and the truth is not in us."*

And now listen to this verse in Romans 3:23,

> *"For all have sinned and fall short of the glory of God."*

There it is folks, the reason the promise of forgiveness is so important and why we should be so grateful that God sent Jesus, the only sinless man, to die on a cross and take the punishment for our sins.

1 Peter 3:18 says, *"For Christ suffered once for sins, the righteous for the unrighteous, that he might bring us to God."* Sin is a problem for us if we

have a desire that I hope you all have to be welcomed into the Kingdom of Heaven when you pass on from this life, and one thing we all know for sure, we will *all* pass on.

The Bible never tells us that everyone goes to heaven or that good people go to heaven or that church-going people go to heaven. It tells us that righteous people go to heaven. Here is what we need to do to gain this assurance found in 1 John 1:9,

> *"If we confess our sins, He is faithful and just to forgive us our sins, and to cleanse us from all unrighteousness."*

There you go—the promise by God to cleanse us from *all* unrighteousness. In other words, to make us righteous, meaning right with God, so that we can be assured of our eternal destination. And believe it or not, He didn't make it hard for us.

So now let's go on and look at some other verses that relate to the promise of forgiveness.

> *"For you Lord, are good, and ready to forgive. And abundant in mercy to all those who call upon you" (Psalm 86:5, NKJV).*

- Note there are no restrictions. God is ready to answer prayer. He is merciful, not laying down a lot of rules and regulations, and that mercy extends to not just those with money, influence, position in the church, but *all* those who call on Him. How great is that!

> *"Come now, and let us reason together, says the Lord, though your sins are like scarlet, they shall be as white as snow" (Isaiah 1:18).*

- I always love it when God gives me a picture of what He's telling me. I can see it now, can't you? Scarlet versus white. I know what my life was like before I came to the Lord that first time, 31 years ago on April 13th and confessed my sins that were certainly like scarlet, and how blessed and free I felt when I saw them washed away. I was cleansed and white like snow.

> *"For I will forgive their iniquity and their sin I will remember no more" (Jeremiah 31:34, NKJV).* That's how God works. He forgives and then erases our sins like it says in Romans 4:7-8, *"Blessed (fortunate) are they whose transgressions are forgiven, whose sins are covered. Blessed is the man whose sin the Lord will never count against him."*

That, my friends, is what God's forgiveness is like. It's totally forgotten, never to be brought up again. That's what being covered by the shed blood of the Lord means. All we have to do is "Repent and believe," like the Bible says. In other words, confess that you are a sinner and turn away from that sin to Jesus, and believe that you have been forgiven and redeemed, that you were lost but have now been bought back, as we read in Ephesians 1:7 (NKJV),

> *"In Him we have redemption through His blood, the forgiveness of sins, according to the riches of His grace."*

So, why are we in such a mess? Why are we upside down? Why is there so much chaos everywhere? Well, we live in a sinful world that has turned it's back on God. How I wish people would stop denying He exists, denying that the Bible is the inspired Word of God, and denying that His way is the best way.

Just imagine if the world lived like Jesus taught and lived! Does God want to save our world? Listen to this one last promise I leave you with today

> *"If my people who are called by My name will humble themselves, and pray and seek My face, and turn from their*

wicked ways, then I will hear from heaven, and will forgive their sin and heal their land" (2 Chronicles 7:14, NKJV).

The answer to that question is *yes* God *does* want to save our world, but we have a part to play. Here I am talking to those who claim to be a part of the family of God. We need to humble ourselves, pray, seek God, and turn from our wicked ways. Forgiveness and salvation are available to us as individuals and to our world in general. That's God's promise, and I'm *so* glad it is.

The next promise we will look at is closely connected to this one. Once we're forgiven, we receive an amazing gift.

Question #25

WHAT PROMISE COMES WITH FORGIVENESS?

In this chapter, we move along to see the blessing we receive following our promise of being forgiven of our sins: God will provide us with His Holy Spirit.

Let's begin in Genesis 1:1 where we first see the Holy Spirit mentioned,

> *"In the beginning, God created the heavens and the earth. Now the earth was formless and empty, darkness was over the surface of the deep and the Spirit of God was hovering over the waters."*

He, the Spirit of God, has been with God the Father and God the Son from the beginning.

If we were to journey through the Old Testament, we would see Him involved in a variety of situations, but I'd like to move along to the New Testament to the time of Jesus' baptism by John the Baptist. Listen to Matthew's description of that event in Matthew 3:16,

> *"As soon as Jesus was baptized, he went up out of the water. At that moment heaven was opened, and he saw the Spirit of God descending like a dove and lighting on him. And a voice from heaven said 'This is my Son, whom I love, with him I am well pleased.' Then Jesus was led by the Spirit into the desert to be tempted by the devil."*

Now this isn't the first mention of the involvement of the Spirit. Back in Matthew 1:18 we read,

> *"This is how the birth of Jesus Christ came about: His mother Mary was pledged to be married to Joseph, but before they came together, she was found to be with child through the Holy Spirit."*

I think it's important to note that the Holy Spirit is very much involved in all of the memorable events in the Bible, and because of that the promise, we will receive Him ourselves—this is super encouraging!

Listen to Jesus' words as He is comforting His disciples who are greatly troubled at His teaching that He will soon be leaving them. He tells them in John 14:25-26,

> *"All this I have spoken while still with you. But the counselor, the Holy Spirit, whom the Father will send in my name, will teach you all things and will remind you of everything I have said to you."*

And later in 16:7-8, 12-13 He tells them,

> *"But I tell you the truth: it is good that I am going away. Unless I go away, the Counselor will not come to you; but if I go, I will send him to you. I have much more to say to you, more than you can now bear. But when he, the Spirit of truth, comes, he will guide you into all truth."*

That was truly good news for His followers! They would need this guidance, just as we do today.

In Acts 2:1-3 we read,

> *"When the day of Pentecost came, they were all together (those same disciples) in one place. Suddenly a sound like the blowing of a violent wind came from heaven and filled the whole house where they were sitting. They saw what seemed*

> *to be tongues of fire that separated and came to rest on each of them. All of them were filled with the Holy Spirit."*

Romans 8 is titled, "Life Through the Spirit." This chapter shows how coming into a relationship with Christ Jesus is where we are indwelt by God the Holy Spirit, just like the disciples. This a wonderful chapter I would encourage you to study and believe.

Peter explains it this way in Acts 2:38,

> *"Repent (meaning confess we are sinners) and be baptized, every one of you in the name of Jesus Christ for the forgiveness of your sins. And you will receive the gift of the Holy Spirit."*

That is what the term "born again" means, we are made new—born of the Spirit. We are indwelt by God. Imagine, the One Who loves us more than we can ever conceive indwells us from that point on and will provide us with what the Bible tells us is the Fruit of the Spirit and the Gifts of the Spirit.

In Galatians 5:22-23, the *Fruits of the Spirit* are listed: *love, joy, peace, patience, kindness, goodness, faithfulness, gentleness and self-control.* This promise follows a list of rather terrible acts that before our change we may have participated in (Galatians 5:19-21), it says, *"those who live like this will not inherit the kingdom of Heaven."* That is what we are saved out of—those acts of our sinful nature—by the change that comes through the indwelling of the Holy Spirit.

We all receive the Fruit of the Spirit, however, as we move along to look at the Gifts of the Spirit, God provides each of us with different gifts at different times in order to fulfill the will of God for the common good.

In 1 Corinthians 12, we see how this works and that as it says in verse 4, "*There are different kinds of gifts but the same Spirit"* Those different gifts include wisdom, knowledge, faith, healing, prophecy, miraculous powers, discernment, speaking in tongues, interpretation of tongues, serving, giving, teaching and mercy. And in verse 11 says,

> *"All these are the work of one and the same spirit and he gives them to each one, just as He determines."*

So, this promise of the Holy Spirit is amazing and once we become a child of God, connected to Him by faith in Jesus Christ, we are indwelt by this blessed Holy Spirit. I hope you have come to the place where you'd like to be free from your sinful nature and move into the family of God and be led by His Spirit.

Question #26

HOW DOES GOD GIVE US A CHANGED HEART?

Following our look at the promise that we can be totally forgiven and are provided with the indwelling of God the Holy Spirit, it seems only fitting that in this chapter we move along to see His promise of a changed heart.

I don't know about you but looking back on my life before Jesus became my Savior and I was indwelt by God the Holy Spirit, I see my heart was in bad shape.

Let's see what condition in general the heart is in prior to God's change:

> *"The LORD saw that the wickedness of man was great in the earth, and that every intent of the thoughts of his heart was only evil continually." –Genesis 6:5, NKJV*

> *"The heart is deceitful above all things, and desperately sick; who can understand it?" –Jeremiah 17:9, NASB*

The result is in Mark 7:21-23,

> *"For from within, out of men's hearts, come evil thoughts, sexual immorality, theft, murder, adultery, greed, malice, deceit, lewdness, envy, slander, arrogance and folly. All these evils come from inside and make a man 'unclean.'"*

Here is where we thank God as we see in 1 John 1:9,

> *"If we confess our sins, he is faithful and just to forgive us our sins and to cleanse us from all unrighteousness."*

As the Bible tells us in Romans 3:23, *"We have all sinned and fall short of the Glory of God"*

A new and cleansed heart which is where sin comes from is a wonderful gift promised by God in His Word. I remember shortly after my conversion, there was a time when I wondered if I really was saved. So, I went to the Christian Bookstore to see if I could find out for sure. After looking around, I came upon a book titled, *The Change Factor.* It wasn't a big book, so when I took it to the counter to pay for it, I was amazed at how expensive it was! But I decided God must have led me to choose it from the shelf, so I paid the price and set off home to read.

The Scripture verse that provided all the answers I needed was right there as a subtitle,

> *The Change Factor, 2 Corinthians 5:17 "Therefore if anyone is in Christ, he is a new creation, old things have passed away, behold, all things have become new."*

I recognized right away that this was me. My old thoughts, words, habits, and behaviours had definitely passed away. All things had become new including my heart. From that day forward, I never doubted again. I knew God had changed me and I was in Christ.

Galatians 2:20 shows us Paul's testimony concerning this change.

> *"I have been crucified with Christ and I no longer live, but Christ lives in me. And the life which I now live in the flesh I live by faith in the Son of God, who loved me and gave himself for me."*

But there are others.

Let's go back into the Old Testament to the book of Jeremiah and see God's promises for those who had been taken into exile by Babylon. Here is what Jeremiah was told,

"My eyes will watch over them for their good, and I will bring them back to this land. I will build them up and not tear them down. I will plant them and not uproot them. I will give them a (new) heart to know me, that I am the LORD" (Jeremiah 24:6-7).

Did that happen? Yes, yes it did.

We also see a similar promise of a changed heart given to Ezekiel,

"I will give them an undivided heart and put a new spirit in them; I will remove from them their heart of stone and give them a heart of flesh. Then they will follow my decrees and be careful to keep my laws. They will be my people and I will be their God" (Ezekiel 11:19-20).

God is reinforcing a basic truth that we all need a changed heart if we're going to follow Him and He promises to provide it when we come to Him, repentant and ready to follow Him.

In closing, let's take a look at what a person with a changed heart looks like.

First of all, we will recognize our need of God Proverbs 3: 5-6 (ESV) tells us,

"Trust in the LORD with all your heart, and do not lean on your own understanding. In all your ways acknowledge him, and he will make straight your paths."

Then we will seek Him with all our heart. Psalm 119: 1-2 tells us,

"Blessed (or fortunate) are those whose ways are blameless, who walk according to the law of the LORD. Blessed are those who keep his statutes and seek him with all their heart."

We will store up or memorize God's Word like the Psalmist says,

> *"I have stored up your word in my heart, that I might not sin against you" (Psalms 119:11, ESV)* as a way of protection against sin.

God Himself will provide us with desires that are according to His will. Psalm 37:4 (ESV)

> *"Delight yourself in the LORD, and he will give you the desires of your heart"*

We don't want to ask for things in opposition to God's will so come to Him asking only for what He's laid on your heart.

I'd like to close with this wonderful promise from the beatitudes in Matthew 5:8,

> *"Blessed are the pure in heart, for they shall see God."*

That, my friends, is a wonderful result of having a changed heart, of having a heart made pure by God's indwelling Spirit. We are blessed and we will see God. This is my hope for you.

Question #27

DOES GOD PROMISE US VICTORY OVER SIN?

As I considered this promise, I was drawn to the progression of this series and how each of the teachings have built up to this truth. I think you'll agree as we do a quick review:

- All the promises of God are true
- God has the power to accomplish what He says He will
- God promises to answer prayer
- God promises to guide us and to strengthen us
- He gives us the assurance of His forgiveness
- He provides us with The Holy Spirit and a Changed Heart

We have the assurance of being cleansed from our sins and filled with God's Spirit and blessed with a changed heart. But you might ask, how can I be assured that I won't fall prey to the Devil's schemes again or that I won't fall back into a sinful life.

That is what we'll look at today, God's promise for victory over sin.

I don't know about you, but that's good news! Let's look at some Scripture that affirms this truth. God doesn't leave us to deal with the Devil's attacks on our own; we will have protection provided by our faith as we see in the following verses:

> *"Above all, taking the shield of faith wherewith ye shall be able to quench all the fiery darts of the evil one." –Ephesians 6:16*

This is a very clear picture of our ability to put out or quench the attack of the enemy. Picture Paul's teaching in this section of us being dressed in armor. Here we have a shield out front of us, a shield of faith that is our protection. Great news—right?

> *"And the God of peace will crush Satan under your feet shortly. The grace of our Lord Jesus Christ be with you. –Romans 16:20, NKJV*

> *"For it is God who works in you both to will and to do for His good pleasure." –Philippians 2:13*, NKJV

> *"So I say, live by the Spirit, and you will not gratify the desires of the sinful nature." –Galatians 5:16*

> *"For everyone born of God overcomes the world. This is the victory that has overcome the world, even our faith" (1John 5:4).*

To overcome the world is to gain victory over our sinful pattern of life. God gives us the strength once we come into a personal relationship with Him by faith.

And now I'd like to close with what I believe sums up the totality of this protection:

> *"Yet in all these things we are more than conquerors through Him who loved us. For I am persuaded that neither death nor life, nor angels nor principalities, nor powers, nor things present nor things to come, nor height nor depth, nor any other created thing, shall be able to separate us from the love of God which is in Christ Jesus our Lord." –Romans 8:37-39, NKJV*

Because it uses the term "in all things," we have the assurance that we are even more than conquerors. But Paul doesn't stop there. He shows us the totality of God's loving reach.

I think that pretty well sums up the teaching on the promise of victory over sin.

However, there is one more piece of advice I'd like you to remember in all of this. We have a part to play in this promise:

> *"Do not conform any longer to the pattern of this world but be transformed by the renewing of your mind. Then you will be able to test and approve what God's will is—his good, pleasing and perfect will." –Romans 12:2*

I hope you have been encouraged in this teaching on the promises of God. I pray you feel secure in the love and protection of God, because of your relationship with the Son, Jesus the Christ.

In the closing 3 chapters of this book, I want to leave you with promises about our future and our eternal life. Jesus Christ is coming back and a picture of just what our world will look like when He does.

A bright and wonderful future awaits us!

QUESTIONS ABOUT OUR FUTURE

Question #28

DO WE HAVE A PROMISE OF ETERNAL LIFE?

In the last 9 chapters, we've been focusing on how we can not only trust God's promises but how important they are in our everyday lives.

We now move along to the closing section of this book, moving ahead to our future. It's very important to know not only Who holds our future but also what our future looks like.

God wants us to know and be prepared for the promise of eternal life.

Would you agree that our culture is obsessed with longevity? While it's natural to desire many healthy years on earth, we must however remind ourselves that life doesn't end with physical death. The true issue is our *eternal destiny.*

We will understand more clearly where we go after our life is over in this chapter. There is only one way to be assured that we are destined for life in heaven and the choices we make in the here and now are what matter.

After death, there is no mercy or grace that can bridge the gap between hell and heaven. The matter must be settled while we are alive on earth. Be encouraged from this passage spoken by Jesus

> *"For God so loved the world, that he gave His only begotten son, that whosoever believeth in Him shall have everlasting life" (John 3:16).*

And listen to Paul in Romans 10:9 as he expounds on this call to believe *"that if you confess with your mouth, 'Jesus is Lord,' and believe in your heart that God raised Him from the dead, you will be saved."*

In other words, you can be blessed with eternal life in heaven. So, let's begin by looking into the Scriptures where we will find a wonderful array of affirmations from Jesus' own lips as well as those who followed Him that I hope will encourage you to not only nod your head in agreement but to say, "Yes, Lord Jesus, I believe, and I want to live with You in heaven forever."

Listen once again to Jesus in John 5:24,

"I tell you the truth, whoever hears my word and believes in him who sent me has eternal life and will not be condemned, he has crossed over from death to life."

Later in 1 John 5:13 in the closing portion of John's letter to believers, he gives them this assurance,

"I write these things to you who believe in the name of the Son of God so that you may know that you have eternal life."

A message that was as important to the early Christians as it is for us today.

Here is a passage where Jesus addresses His followers as His sheep

"My sheep listen to my voice; I know them, and they follow me. I give them eternal life and they shall never perish; no one can snatch them out of my hand" (John 10:27-28).

Wow what a wonderful promise! We can be safe and secure in the arms of the Good Shepherd, not just for our journey here on earth, but forever!

And then in the very next chapter, Jesus says,

> *"I am the resurrection and the life. He who believes in me will live, even though he dies; and whoever lives and believes in me will never die"* (John 11:25-26).

So, you might ask, what will we look like when we enter eternal life? If you were to go to the Gospel of John and read what Jesus was like following His resurrection, you'll get a wonderful idea of what we have in store.

In Philippians 3:20-21 we hear Paul share this truth,

> *"Our citizenship is in heaven. And we eagerly await a Saviour from there, the Lord Jesus Christ; who, by the power that enables him to bring everything under his control, will transform our lowly bodies so that they will be like his glorious body."*

There are so many passages I could share with you that confirm the wonderful truth that God has prepared a way for us to live with Him forever which, by the way, was His intention back in the book of Genesis when He walked with His creation in the Garden—before the fall.

I hope you are looking forward to the eternal life God has prepared for us. I would imagine as we continue to try and endure this upside-down world, this is sure wonderful news.

In Chapter 29 we ask is Jesus really coming back? with the wonderful answer: Yes! He is!

Question #29

IS JESUS REALLY COMING BACK?

This too is a Promise.

The Bible verses we will look at to answer our question are actually promises as well. The fact that He is coming back is not just good news, it's *wonderful* news!

Let's begin our journey by listening to Jesus Himself and many of the biblical writers as they confirm the answer I shared earlier—Jesus *is* coming back.

In Matthew 24:3, Jesus is asked by the disciples

> *"Tell us', they said, 'when will this happen and what will be the sign of your coming and of the end of the age?'"*

Here is His answer in Matthew 24:27, 30,

> *"For as lightning that comes from the east is visible even in the west, so will be the coming of the Son of Man (a phrase that Jesus uses often to describe himself)...At that time the sign of the Son of Man will appear in the sky, and all the nations of the earth will mourn. They will see the Son of Man coming on the clouds of the sky and power and great glory."*

We also hear Jesus tell us in John 14:2-3 where He is comforting His disciples as he is preparing to leave them.

> *"In my Father's house are many rooms, if it were not so, I would have told you. I am going there to prepare a place*

for you. And if I go and prepare a place for you, I will come back and take you to be with me that you also may be where I am."

Again, He tells us in Revelation 3:11,

"I am coming soon. Hold on to what you have, so that no one will take your crown."

Later He says in Revelation 16:15,

"Behold I come like a thief! Blessed is he who stays awake and keeps his clothes with him so that he may not go naked and be shamefully exposed."

Now I know we could stop right here after listening to the truth that He will return as spoken by Jesus Himself, however, I feel it's important to share with you some other references to this truth from the lips of John, Angels, Paul, Peter, Titus, Jude and others. This is not a secret being kept from us.

John's vision is recorded in Revelation 1:7-8,

"Look, he is coming with the clouds, and every eye will see him, even those who pierced him; and all the peoples of the earth will mourn, because of him. So shall it be! Amen."

Words from the Angels to those at the transfiguration

"Men of Galilee,' they said, 'why do you stand here looking into the sky? This same Jesus, who has been taken from you into heaven, will come back in the same way you have seen him go into heaven'" (Acts 1:11).

Here are Paul's words to believers,

"When Christ, who is your life, appears, then you also will appear with him in glory" (Colossians 3:4).

And he also tells us in Philippians 3:20,

> *"But our citizenship is in heaven. And we eagerly await a Savior from there, the Lord Jesus Christ."*

And again in 1 Corinthians 1:7,

> *"Therefore do not lack any spiritual gift as you eagerly wait for our Lord Jesus Christ to be revealed."*

Peter's teaching about the elders being shepherds of God's flock says this,

> *"And when the Chief Shepherd appears, you will receive the crown of glory that will never fade away" (1 Peter 5:4).*

John says to believers,

> *"Dear friends, now we are children of God, and what we will be has not yet been made known. But we know that when he appears, we shall be like him, for we shall see him as he is" (1 John 3:2).*

Titus proclaims what his followers must teach

> *"while we wait for the blessed hope—the glorious appearing of our great God and Saviour, Jesus Christ" (Titus 2:13).*

The writer of Hebrews tells us,

> *"Just as man is destined to die once, and after that to face judgment, so Christ was sacrificed once to take away the sins of many people; and he will appear a second time, not to bear sin, but to bring salvation to those who are waiting for him" (Hebrews 9:27-28).*

Jude takes us back to the Old Testament,

> *"Enoch, the seventh from Adam, prophesied about these men: 'See the Lord is coming with thousands upon thousands of his holy ones to judge everyone, and to convict all the ungodly of all the ungodly acts they have done in the ungodly way, and of all the harsh words ungodly sinners have spoken against him" (Jude 1:14-15).*

Paul, in 1 Thessalonians 4, in a section titled "The Coming of the Lord," is quite clear that Jesus is returning,

> *"For the Lord himself will come down from heaven, with a loud command, with the voice of the archangel and with the trumpet call of God, and the dead in Christ will rise first"* (verse 16), and then in 5:2, *"For you know very well that the day of the Lord will come like a thief in the night."*

James provides teaching under the heading "Patience in Suffering" James 5:8,

> *"You too, be patient and stand firm because the Lord's coming is near."*

In closing, I'd like to leave you once again with the words of Jesus in the closing chapter of the Bible, Revelation 22:20,

> *"Yes, I am coming soon."*

John's response is, *"Amen, Come, Lord Jesus."* That, my friends, is my response as well! During this time of chaos, trying to cope with this upside-down world, I believe there is only one true answer—the return of Jesus Christ.

That is why I have chosen to end this book by looking what our world will look like when He does return.

Question #30

WHAT WILL OUR WORLD LOOK LIKE WHEN HE RETURNS?

Now let's see what God has had planned for us and our world from the very beginning.

It's important for us to remember that the Bible begins at Genesis 1, not at Genesis 3. It doesn't begin with the problem of sin; it begins with the beauty of the earth, and God remains committed to His creation, in the light of this. God, not Satan, will have the final victory over what God has made. It will not be discarded but rescued.

Therefore, it's not surprising that Scripture talks of the fulfillment of this rescue as "a new heaven and a new earth."

Here are a few places in the Old Testament and the New Testament where we hear about this.

> *"Behold, I will create new heavens and a new earth. The former things will not be remembered, nor will they come to mind."–Isaiah 65:17*

> *"As the new heavens and the new earth that I make will endure before Me,' declares the Lord, 'so will your name and descendants endure.'"–Isaiah 66:22*

> *"But in keeping with his promise we are looking forward to a new heaven and a new earth, the home of righteousness."–2 Peter 3:13*

How exciting it is to see how the story of the Bible doesn't only begin with,

> *"God created the heavens and the earth" (Genesis 1:1) but* ends with John declaring *"then I saw a new heaven and the new earth" (Revelation 21:1).*

Now let's consider God's remedy for what happened in the Garden of Eden and how it resulted in the suffering that pervades every part of our lives. Throughout the Bible, God shows His commitment to fix this problem by descending to earth. This actually begins in Eden where He walks with Adam in the garden (Genesis 3:8) and it continues as God's glory is beheld in the tabernacle in the temple, in the incarnation, in the crucifixion, in the resurrection and in the gift of the Holy Spirit.

However, when Jesus returns, it will not be just for a visit, to pick us up and take us elsewhere. *He is coming to stay.* The New Jerusalem will descend to earth and the beauty of God's creation will be restored and renewed.

Think of it this way, the Creation found in Genesis and the New Creation in Revelation are bookends of the Bible. God is concerned for the renewal of this earth and has a plan.

Let's consider Israel, often referred to as the Holy Land throughout the Old Testament as it comes to a close. The people of Israel had returned from Babylonian captivity and were re-establishing themselves in the land, but they were still awaiting a Messiah who would accomplish God's purposes.

As the New Testament opens, we are introduced to this Messiah. Jesus fulfills all the promises of God and the transition from a holy land to a holy earth begins.

The ultimate realization of this will be seen in the new heavens and a new earth in which righteousness dwells as we see in 2 Peter 3:13,

> *"But in keeping with his promise we are looking forward to a new heaven and a new earth, the home of righteousness."*

So how does all this affect our destiny? Let's consider Jesus' resurrection. Jesus was raised to earth, not to heaven. We should not confuse the resurrection and the ascension. The grave where His body was placed following His crucifixion was empty. After His resurrection, Jesus's body was clearly transformed, but it was still the very same physical body that was laid in the tomb. This resurrection is described as the firstfruits of the general resurrection in *1 Corinthians 15:20-23,*

> *"But Christ has indeed been raised from the dead, the firstfruits of those who have fallen asleep (died). For since death came through a man, the resurrection of the dead comes also through a man. For as in Adam all die, so in Christ all will be made alive. But each in his own turn: Christ, the firstfruits; then, when he comes, those who belong to him."*

Our bodies will also be raised in a way that will allow us to live in the new heavens and the new earth. We do not know all the details of what this will look like, but we know that "we shall be like Him" (1 John 3:2).

We are also provided a wonderful clear declaration of this truth about a new heaven and new earth (when Jesus returns) in Revelation 21:1-5,

> *"Then I saw a new heaven and a new earth, for the first heaven and the first earth had passed away, and there was no longer any sea. I saw the Holy City, the new Jerusalem, coming down out of heaven from God, prepared as a bride beautifully dressed for her husband. And I heard a loud voice from the throne saying, 'Now the dwelling of God is with men, and he will live with them. They will be his people, and God himself will be with them, and be their God. He will wipe every tear from their eyes. There will be no more death or mourning or crying or pain, for the old order of things has passed away.' He who was seated on the throne said, 'I am making everything new!' Then he said, 'Write this down, for these words are trustworthy and true.'"*

I want to encourage you to go to Revelation 21:10 and take a journey through chapter 22:1-6 and be amazed at what our future holds. I told you it would be good news!

I love how these sections close with instructions to write these things down because they are true. In Revelation 21:5 and 22:6. Maybe you might remember way back in Chapter 2 we looked at the question "Is there somewhere I can go to find out about God that is trustworthy and true?" And that we were assured, yes there is, and here is that confirmation once again.

In closing, I want to make sure you understand just what God has planned for those who commit their lives to Jesus. That is how we can be sure we will have a place in this amazing new creation God has planned for us. The glorious promise of God is that this earth will be made new. This will be a reversal of the curse of Eden.

The present order of creation will be replaced in this new order where the only people who exist will be God's people. They will live in the closest of relationships with God once again, just as Adam and Eve once did.

I think it's appropriate to close with Jesus' words found in the closing chapter of Revelation and the reference to the Tree of Life that Adam and Eve had been banished from by God back in Genesis 3.

> *"Behold, I am coming soon! My reward is with me, and I will give to everyone according to what he has done. I am the Alpha and the Omega, the First and the Last, the Beginning and the End. Blessed are those who wash their robes, that they may have the right to the tree of life and may go through the gates into the city." –Revelation 22:12-14*

Amen!

ACKNOWLEDGEMENT

How can I close this book without remembering those who have helped me in so many ways.

- My Lord and Saviour, Jesus Christ
- My husband, Wayne, who without his support, encouragement and help it would have never been completed. He was always available to serve as my main sounding board for the ideas expressed in this book with sage and godly advise.
- I dedicate this writing In memory of our mothers, Patricia and Rose, who honoured their commitment to raise us in a Christian home and maintained a godly influence even when we rebelled.
- I also dedicate this, my first book, to my friends and family in The Salvation Army who welcomed a lost and confused young woman into their midst and led us into Ministry through their teaching, encouragement and support.

www.ingramcontent.com/pod-product-compliance
Ingram Content Group UK Ltd.
Pitfield, Milton Keynes, MK11 3LW, UK
UKHW020424250726
13967UKWH00007B/2801